Amazon Ads to Sell More Books: 2022 Edition

Book Marketing for Indie Authors

Alana J. Terry

Published by Successful Writer Academy, 2022.

AMAZON ADS TO SELL MORE BOOKS: 2022 EDITION

First edition. March 1, 2022.

ISBN: 979-8201721992

Written by Alana J. Terry.

Table of Contents

Skyrocket Your Career with Amazon Ads

If you're a published author, do you remember receiving your very first royalty check? My debut novel was a Christian suspense set in North Korea, and my first royalty check came in the mail from KDP and was $11.32. It was hardly enough to buy myself a pastry and cup of fancy coffee, but I felt so proud because that money came from my book!

It was the same feeling the very first time I got a sale from an Amazon ad back in the fall of 2017. I couldn't believe it. I sat there staring at my dashboard. I paid Amazon about 13 cents to get a click, and as a result of that click, a casual browser became a paying customer.

Just like that.

Since then, I've spent well over a hundred thousand dollars on Amazon ads. More importantly, I've earned far more money back from those ads than I've spent. Before I started running Amazon ads, I was making about a thousand dollars in royalties a month. If I got a Bookbub deal or had a new release, it might be a little more. It was enough for me to hire a cover designer and editor so I could keep writing more books, and that was about it.

Once I learned how to scale up my ads, I started seeing regular five-figure months. This increased revenue allowed me to support my family, take a fiction Sabbatical in 2020 (and still make more profit than any other year), purchase our dream home, and still have money to continue running ads and support my writing business.

No matter how much you're bringing in from your writing income now, I bet you'd be excited to see that number double. Or triple ...

Or more!

The amazing thing about Amazon ads is that you've already done the work. You've already written your manuscript, commissioned your cover, paid your editor, and published your book. Amazon ads just ensure that more people see the masterpiece you've created.

Common Objections

If you were to ask authors why they're not running Amazon ads, you might hear one of these responses. Maybe you've even said something like this in the past!

1) **I shouldn't have to pay Amazon to promote my book.** Amazon ads, according to some authors, is just a way for Amazon to steal money from authors. Instead of thinking about it as a way Amazon's trying to rip you off, think about it as a way to partner with them for extra visibility.

Remember when authors would do nearly anything to get organic visibility on Amazon? Now we can buy visibility and make more money while we're doing it, and the end result can be empowering like we just mentioned.

Other authors figure that if they're book is good enough, people will find it without the need for paid ads. Well, if you believe your book truly is that great, then your goal should be to get it in front of as many possible readers as you can, and Amazon ads are a very effective way to do just that.

2) **I don't have money to spend on ads.** I've got good news for you! Amazon ads don't have to be expensive. My first ads were all set up with $5 a day budgets. I didn't increase my spending until I actually started seeing the profit. Once I realized how easy it was to turn my $5 a day into $10 or $20 or $30, it wasn't hard or scary to invest more money into ads.

3) **I don't have time to learn a new platform.** Some authors avoid Amazon ads because they don't want to spend time on marketing. They just want to write more books. In addition to running Amazon ads, I've also run a lot of Facebook ads and Bookbub cost-per-click ads, and you'll be happy to learn that Amazon ads are by far the quickest to both set up and maintain. If I had to guess, on a given month I probably spend three or four hours on Amazon ads. I'll create new ads and then just check in with my ads dashboard from my phone when I want to review my numbers.

4) **Aren't ads really hard and confusing to set up?** The biggest reason I avoided Amazon ads at first was because I was intimidated at the thought of learning a whole new dashboard. Once I learned what the different terms meant and how to analyze my results, I realized ads weren't complicated at all. That's why I wrote this book, to give you a step-by-step companion so you can dive into ads with confidence.

Sound good? I can't wait to get started!

Benefits of Amazon Ads

Amazon ads can be great for your monthly revenue and help you meet your wildest income goals, but there are quite a few other benefits of running Amazon ads in addition to direct sales.

1) **Visibility.** Amazon ads (especially the sponsored ads, which will be the focus of this book) are *everywhere*, and for authors they are great for visibility. Who is the household name in your genre, the author whose new releases always spike to the top of the charts? Imagine that every time somebody does a search for Famous Author Dude or goes to buy Famous Author Dude's newest release, that reader also sees your book being promoted!

Even cooler is the fact that you aren't paying Amazon for this added visibility. Amazon only charges you when somebody *clicks* on your ad, but hundreds of thousands of people will see your featured ads without clicking. That's hundreds of thousands of readers who have seen a glimpse of your cover ... and you don't pay for that extra exposure. It's like Amazon giving you free billboard space!

2) **Eager readers.** Amazon ads allow you to target readers where they're most likely to buy ... when they're already shopping in the Kindle store. This makes them different from any other ad platform. When somebody is scrolling through Facebook, for example, they aren't looking to buy a book. If they happen to see a Facebook ad for a book and click it, they might decide to make a purchase, but that's not why they're on Facebook.

By contrast, if somebody is on an Amazon sales page, there's a very high chance that they're there because they're looking for something to read. This means it usually takes fewer clicks to make a sale on Amazon than on any other dashboard.

3) **Data, data, data.** When you run Amazon ads, you can learn a lot about your book and your ideal readers.

Let's say you run three different ads targeting Authors A, B, and C. Author C gives you an amazing number of clicks and sales. You can assume that Author C's readers are going to love your books, and you can use that information to make smart marketing decisions for your books. Maybe you target Author C in your Facebook or Bookbub click ads (if you choose to dive into these platforms). Maybe you reach out to Author C on social media and do a promotion together. Maybe you just keep on targeting Author C in your Amazon ads, and every time C has a new book out, you make sure your title appears on that sales page.

We'll get into numbers and analysis in later parts of this book, but the data you get from running Amazon ads is priceless. In addition to guiding your marketing decisions as in the examples above, the data you get from your ads dashboard can also impact the way you publish. Imagine you have two different covers and don't know which one readers will like more. Or say you're considering changing your book's blurb to see if that will increase sales.

By running Amazon ads and tracking your data over time, you'll be able to decide with mathematical and statistical precision whether or not these changes to your book's sales page help or hinder your sales.

4) **Non-monetary benefits.** Most of us are running Amazon ads because we want to make a profit, and this book is going to show you how to do just that. But sometimes I choose to let an ad run even with a small profit margin. It's not always just about the money.

Let's say you are running ads for your title *Best Debut Ever.* You spend a dollar in ads and you make a dollar back in book sales.

Some people would give up and say your ads aren't working.

But you are patient and willing to take a slow-burn approach to your writing. You keep these ads going, you budget responsibly, and even though you're only breaking even, you're still getting a *lot* of added benefits.

First of all, the more readers you have, the higher your sales rank will be. Your title will be more likely to appear in also-boughts for other authors in your genre. Organic sales will increase, and Amazon's algorithm will start promoting your book for free.

Second of all, the more people who buy and read your book, the more reviews you're likely to receive. Reviews are great social proof for your title and will increase your sales down the road. They also make it more likely that your book will be selected by other promotional sites who have competitive standards for the books they advertise (hello, Bookbub editorial team!).

Additionally, even if all you're doing is breaking even on *Best Debut Ever*, if *Best Debut Ever* really is that great of a book, you'll have the added benefit of gaining lifelong fans. These readers will go on to buy and read your other titles, spread the word to their friends, join your mailing list, etc. In other words, even though we're diving into Amazon ads for the purpose of making a profit, there are a ton of side benefits that can't be measured using a simple formula.

5) **Confidence.** When I was a new author, the only way I got a big increase in sales was if I was fortunate enough for the Bookbub editorial team to select my book for a featured deal. I felt like I was a victim to every single change in Amazon's visibility rules, and my success was based more on luck than anything else.

Once you learn how to run ads, you get to determine your own success trajectory. There's no gatekeeper telling you if your book is good enough to promote, and the number of potential new readers on Amazon is approaching limitless.

Why NOW is the Time to Run Amazon Ads

The first edition of this book was released in early 2019, when clicks were (in general) cheaper than they are today. Maybe you've been around in the author space long enough that you've heard people talking about getting two- or three-cent clicks on their Amazon ads. With numbers that low, it's almost impossible not to make a big stinking profit!

Amazon ads are getting more expensive as more and more authors are using the platform. That's okay. Actually, in some ways it's a good thing.

Look at it this way. If any and every writer/publisher could get clicks for two or three cents using Amazon ads, then basically anybody could make a profit. As a result, everybody and their grandma would be clamoring to use that platform. The books being advertised wouldn't have to meet any real quality standards because, like I said, with clicks that cheap it's almost impossible not to make a profit.

Now, with clicks costing an average of 50 cents or more (varying widely by genre and keyword, of course), the only people who are going to be using and continuing to use Amazon ads are the authors who have professional covers and great books that can still be cost-effective to advertise at the more competitive prices. Consequently, readers will see a higher quality of books being promoted when they're browsing on Amazon, which will result in a net gain for authors everywhere.

Bottom line? Clicks were cheaper when Amazon ads first rolled out, but don't let that stop you from learning Amazon ads today. To use a somewhat glib, albeit poignant, riddle, let me ask you this. Do you know when the best time is to plant a tree?

Answer: Twenty years ago.

Do you know the second best time to plant a tree?

Answer: Today.

It's very unlikely that Amazon clicks will get cheaper than they are right now. The days of authors seeing single-cent clicks aren't coming back, barring some sort of strange economic catastrophe (in which case, who's going to bother advertising on Amazon anyway?).

Do you know what is likely, however?

That as more and more authors dive into Amazon ads, click rates will continue to go up.

So jump in now! For those of you who own cars, you'll understand that it's like gas prices. Do you remember a time when paying $2.50 for a gallon of gas felt like highway robbery? But now we'd all love to see rates that low. It's all a matter of perspective and what side of history you're standing on.

So don't be the author who looks back five years from now and says, "Wow, I wish I had learned Amazon ads before they were a dollar a click!" Dive in now and invest in learning. Your efforts will be well worth it, and this book is your straightforward step-by-step guide to get started.

Different Types of Ads

I'm sure you've *heard* about Amazon ads (unless you've been sequestered away in a cell working on the Great American Novel for twenty hours a day). In fact, you've probably even heard that running ads on Amazon is a really important part of many authors' success.

But as it turns out, there are quite a few different types of Amazon ads, so before we dive into how to set your own ads up, it's important to know what we're talking about.

Which brings us to our brief vocabulary lesson. A lot of people think vocabulary is boring, but you're an author, so obviously you don't.

Right?

Good.

Let's dive into what the different types of Amazon ads are.

Lockscreen Ads

Good news. This kind of ad will *not* appear on the test. Know why? Because lockscreen ads in general don't work very well, and I don't recommend using them.

Lockscreen ads are the ads shown to Kindle readers when they unlock their devices. If you have a Kindle ereader, you know exactly what we're talking about. Think of it as the screensaver for your Kindle. This image you see is an ad.

On the surface, these sound like a smart ad placement, until you talk to basically any author who's used them with no success. One reason for their lack of efficacy probably has to do with the fact that when somebody opens they're Kindle, they're planning to *read* a book, not buy one. That's why in this book we'll focus mostly on sponsored product ads.

Takeaways to Remember:

- Lockscreen ads appear as Kindle screensavers. Your mileage may vary, but in general most authors find these ads are not effective.

- We'll focus mostly on sponsored product ads in this book.

What are Sponsored Product Ads?

Now it's time to talk about my favorite kind of ads: sponsored product ads (which in this book we'll often call sponsored ads for short).

If you have books for sale in the Kindle store, you almost certainly have seen sponsored product ads. These little guys show up just about everywhere. Most commonly, sponsored product ads appear as cover thumbnails (similar to a book's also-boughts) in a carousel that shows book covers, an optional short blurb, the book's price, number of reviews, and average star rating. Because the book cover is such a prominent feature in sponsored ads, it's critically important to choose cover images that stand out well in thumbnail.

A quick note here. When sponsored products (or any type of Amazon ads) first appeared under authors' book listings, authors were understandably upset.

Why would I want Amazon to try to sell *someone else's book* on my book page? It would be like walking into a Coke factory and having the worker behind the front desk asking if I wanted to try free samples of Pepsi.

Why is Amazon giving advertising space on my page to my competitors?" That's what authors were asking. Most of us by now realize that Amazon ads are here to stay. They're on our book pages whether we want them to be or not. But I think the mindset issue is important enough to discuss here before we go on.

If I'm a romance reader and I'm on your book page and I see a sponsored ad for another romance book that looks like it's going to be a great read and I buy that book, the world hasn't ended. Far from it. Because readers read books. Your books, my books, their books ... In other words, just because someone clicks on a sponsored ad and buys someone else's book doesn't mean they're never going to come back and read yours. Right?

So don't get upset about other authors' sponsored ads appearing on your book pages. First of all, there's absolutely nothing you can do to make sponsored ads disappear. Amazon's not going to just turn off sponsored ads when they're making so much money from them. Second of all, the more books readers buy in your genre, the more books are in demand.

Of course, you might worry that if I am a potential reader on your book page, and I see and click on someone else's sponsored ad and go buy their book, you've just lost out on a sale. Instead of getting upset at Amazon for having sponsored ads (which, like I said, earn them tons of money and aren't going anywhere ever), or instead of getting upset with other authors for advertising on your page, think of it as a good reason to make sure you have the best cover and the best blurb possible so no reader would *want* to click away. (It also makes sense for this exact reason to target yourself and your own books, but we'll talk about that in more detail later.)

In addition to the carousel of ads that appear beneath the also-boughts, sponsored ads get other great retail space on Amazon pages.

When you search for a particular author, book, or genre, you'll usually see a headline ad (more on these in a sec), and then beneath that a couple ads with "sponsored" written in small print above the book's title. Other than this one little word, these books look just like all the books that appear beneath it. A reader will see your cover and star rating and will even have the option to buy your book with one-click right then and there.

Let's say a reader is looking for a new series and types "military sci-fi" into Amazon's search bar. And let's say you've set up sponsored ads targeting that particular phrase. This means that your book might be the first book they see beneath the search header. And since readers are used to Amazon's algorithm deciding *everything*, it will look as if your book is one of the top-selling, most popular military sci-fi books in that entire list. So the reader buys your book, which is great news for you because it's a book sale, and great news for the reader because they've just gotten a new book in a genre they were actively searching for.

There are a few other spots where sponsored ads can pop up on product pages, and Amazon seems to change these placements from time to time at random, as any hard-core fans of the now extinct product display ads can testify. You can trust that if Amazon places an ad in a given spot on their product or search pages, they've done the testing to make sure it's in the exact right location to get the most visibility possible. One positive thing to note, as I mentioned earlier, is that you don't pay for Amazon to *show* your ads to readers. You only pay when a reader gives your ad a click, so Amazon's going to put your book in the best places to make sure it's getting the most clicks possible.

It's one example of Amazon's algorithm working in our favor. Yay!

Takeaways to Remember:

- Sponsored product ads appear on product pages of other Kindle books and search pages for certain categories and genres.

- Sponsored product ads show your cover and book rating and sometimes even appear with a one-click buy now button next to them.

- You only pay Amazon when someone clicks on your ad, so Amazon wants to put your book in front of the readers who are most likely to click.

- Sponsored ads aren't going anywhere, so don't waste energy worrying that other people's books appear on your sales page. Just make sure you've got the best covers and blurbs possible so readers won't want to click away.

Headline (aka Sponsored Brand) Ads

I have a guilty pleasure to admit to.

Sometimes when I'm really bored (or discouraged and in want of a pick-me-up), I type *Christian suspense* into the Amazon search bar and see if my books are the first to appear as headline ads on the search page. (It's actually a pretty fun adrenaline rush to see your books show up in the header, then to refresh the page only to find another one of your series in that prime real estate spot.)

Headline ads are officially named *sponsored brand ads*. However, this name can be easily confused with the sponsored product ads I mentioned above. So for the sake of simplicity, we'll stick with calling them headline ads for the remainder of this book.

Headline ads are gorgeous. You can promote an entire series and show off several of your covers in one horizontal bar. If a reader is searching on a laptop, most of the products listed from their search appear beneath the fold (meaning a reader has to scroll down to see them), but your headline ads show up front and center. My headlines ads have a 1.24% click through rate, whereas the click-through rate for my sponsored ads is only 0.063%. And since we're authors here and not mathematicians, I'll simplify for you. WAY more people click on my headline ads than my sponsored ads. No surprise, since one sales page can have over a dozen sponsored ads shown at any given time, whereas a search page has only one headline ad.

There are few bad things about headline ads to mention. The guidelines for uploading an author photo can be a little annoying, and sometimes your ads might get rejected for no good reason, with Amazon telling you that your photo doesn't comply with their rules. They can also sometimes be more expensive (since obviously it's prime real estate).

The good news is that once you've learned how to set up sponsored brand ads, you'll have all the knowledge you need to run headline ads, which is why we're going to keep the focus of this book primarily on sponsored ads.

Takeaways to Remember:

- Headline ads appear as a horizontal bar at the top of search pages, which offers huge visibility and high click-through rates.

- Headline ads require an author photo. Sometimes Amazon can be a little arbitrary about whether they accept your photo or not.

International Ads, Video Ads, and More

Amazon regularly rolls out new options for advertisers. For years, authors could only advertise in the amazon.com (US) store, but now we can run ads in several international marketplaces. Some authors (myself included!) also have experimented with video ads that Amazon seems to be rolling out to certain advertisers.

My recommendation is to start with ads in the US store (since you have the biggest audience to draw from) and stick to simple sponsored product ads. Then, when you've found success there, you can use your knowledge to branch out to international ads, headline ads, and any other type of ad Amazon eventually rolls out.

Takeaways to Remember:

- Once you learn how to run sponsored product ads in the US store (our main focus in this book), you can use the same information to run effective ads in other countries and placements.

Setting Up Sponsored Product Ads

Are you ready to learn how to set up your sponsored product ads? Good! And don't worry. If you're interested in setting up any of the other kinds of ads mentioned previously, once you go through this chapter, you'll have the info you need for that as well! (The set-up instructions for the different types of ads don't vary all that much from one ad to another, which is good news for us.)

I'll be walking you through each step of the Amazon ads dashboard, but if you're more of a visual learner, I have some courses and videos that walk you through setting up ads as well (including the free Amazon Ads Starter Kit which you can get simply by going tohttp://courses.alanaterry.com/kit).

Starting Your Ads

To begin creating ads, you'll need to sign into your KDP account and select the Marketing tab. You'll see an option to select Amazon Ads in different marketplaces. You'll select Amazon.com and click create a campaign.

At that point you'll be able to create one of a few different types of ads. Once you select the type of ad you want to create (in this case a sponsored product), you have the choice to name your ad whatever you want. For the sake of analysis later on, I recommend you include these things in your ad titles:

1) The name of your book and/or series. This can also be an abbreviation. This makes it really easy to search how your ads for one particular book or series are doing without having to sift through a ton of excess data.

2) What you're targeting. We'll talk about targets soon, but your ad name might include auto, genre keywords, author keywords, products, etc.

Additionally, you could also add some of the following data when you name your campaign:

1) The type of ad. I use SP for sponsored product ads (the kind we're talking about) and SB for sponsored brand ads (also known as headline ads). This isn't entirely necessary, because I am able to filter my results fairly easily anyway based on the type of ad, but it's nice to see what kind of ad I'm working with at a glance.

2) The bid price you've set. If you're running the same kind of ads to the same audience with different bids, you'll want to include that data in your title so you know exactly what you're looking at.

3) Anything you're testing. For example, if you're running one ad with a set bid point and running a similar ad where you're allowing Amazon to adjust your bid on your behalf, noting that in your title will make analyzing your results easier in the end.

Here are a few examples of how you could name your ad. Let's say you are advertising book one in your sweet romance series using sponsored product ads. You're targeting authors A, B, and C with your ads, and you're bidding 50 cents a click.

You might choose to name your ad "SR1 – authors A, B, C – 0.50." The SR1 tells you that it's an ad for book one in your sweet romance (SR) series. It also tells you which authors you've targeted and what your bid is.

Another example is as follows. Let's say you're going to run two ads using auto targeting (a cool option Amazon allows for and I'll tell you about soon). Both ads are for your book called *Really Cool Novel*, and you want to see if you'll get better results bidding at 35 cents or 75 cents. So you run two ads and name them "RCN – auto – 0.35" and "RCN – auto – 0.75."

When you pay attention to the way you name your ads, you can then filter your results to get an instant snapshot of how a particular book, series, or audience is working for you.

For example, I always liked setting up ads with auto-generated keywords because it's so quick and easy. This will be the first ad you'll learn how to make from this book, because it takes no time at all.

However, just because an ad is easy to make doesn't make it the best, right? But I can go into my dashboard, search for any ad that has "auto" in the title, and I can see that actually my automatically generated ads are some of my best-performing of all time.

Similarly, if I want to see exactly how one book or one series is doing with ads, as long as I've given all those ads the same identifier in their name, I can filter results to only show me ads for that one book.

Let's go back to your runaway bestseller, *Really Cool Novel*. After your breakaway success with that, you decide to try something totally different and publish *My Life in Poetry*.

Three months later, you're trying to decide if you're going to write more cool novels or more poetic memoirs. So you go to your ads dashboard and search for all ads that have RCN in their name. You discover that for every dollar you spend on ads in that genre, you make two dollars back.

Then you do the same for your poetic memoir ads, which you've given the handy label of MLIP, and you find that for every dollar you spend on ads, you make five dollars back.

That's good news for you if you've got your heart set on writing your life in iambic pentameter!

Now that you've named your ad, it will ask if you want to assign your ad to a portfolio. This is a very nice option for authors who are managing lots of series and/or are very price conscious.

There are two great things you can do with portfolios.

1) Put all your ads for one book or series in a group. This will tell you at a glance how one specific series is performing and can make your analysis a lot simpler.

2) Give your portfolio a budget cap. This is an amount of money that resets each month that you don't want Amazon to overspend. So if you only want to spend $100 a month advertising a certain series, you can put all those ads in a portfolio and give them a $100 limit.

If you're only setting up ads for one book right now, you don't need to make a portfolio (although you could if you want a budget cap). It's also easy to move ads from one portfolio to another, rename your portfolios, or reset your budget limits in the future, so don't stress out too much. In general, the Amazon ads dashboard is fairly forgiving, meaning that most things you want to change are able to be changed.

The only warnings to note about portfolios is that (1) you can't delete a portfolio and (2) if you archive an ad while it's in a portfolio, there's no way to move it out in the future. That's one reason why in general I don't recommend archiving your ads. Just pause the ones you don't want to run. But more on that later!

One more note about portfolios for authors who have run lots of Amazon ads haphazardly in the past. Some authors have taken my Amazon ads course and like the system I'm teaching you here, but it's a little different than what you've done in the past and you don't necessarily want to have all your new ads running alongside all your old ones. What I recommend if you're looking for a "fresh start" for your ads dashboard is to throw all your old ads into one portfolio labeled old ads or something like that, which cleans up your dashboard to only focus on the ones you want to focus on.

That's all about portfolios for now, so now it's time to set your start and end dates as well as your daily budget. For now, it's totally fine to stick with low numbers, especially if you haven't run ads before. If you set a budget of $5 a day, you're not going to break the bank. Even if you run twenty ads with a $5-a-day budget, it's very unlikely Amazon will spend $100.

For example, last week, I started some ads for a new series of Alaskan suspense novels I'd just published. I created 13 ads and set daily budgets of $200 - $250 for each. However, in the past week that the ads have been running, I've only spent a total of $403.55 on these ads. In other words, Amazon will not often spend your *entire* daily budget, and a daily budget as low as $5 can still earn you good results and be great for getting your toes wet on the Amazon advertising platform.

For your start and stop dates, I usually just let the ads run until I decide to turn them off. In general, I don't think you need to worry much about your start and end dates, with these few exceptions:

1) **Preorders**. You CAN run ads for a book that is on preorder. Unless getting a lot of preorder sales is a major part of your marketing strategy, I don't recommend paying for ads on books until they're released. Most people who click on sponsored ads on Amazon are in the mood to buy a book *right now*, so if they click on your book, you'll still get charged but they'll be less likely to buy since your book's not available yet.

If you have a book on preorder, I recommend that you set up your Amazon ads now (so you don't have to worry about them later), but you schedule them to start the day your book goes live.

2) **Sales.** If you're running a 99-cent sale or other kind of price promotion, you might want to have your ads start and stop on the same days as your sale. Let's say you have ads running for a book regularly priced at $4.99. Next week, your book will be 99 cents for three days. If you want to be a data purist, you should really consider pausing the ads you have while your book's at full price, then copying those ads and running them during the three days of your sale. In your ad title for these new ads, you should mention that they're 99 cents. That

way, when you look at your ratio of clicks to sales, you can see exactly how many sales you get per click when the book is 99 cents and how many you get when the book is $4.99.

(Full disclosure: I don't always do this, partly because it takes a lot of time, and partly because I've done it enough times I know my data and conversion rates well enough that I don't have to re-measure them. Also, there's an unspoken rule of thumb with Amazon ads that once you find something that's working well you don't want to mess with it, because Amazon ads as we'll see can behave unpredictably. You don't want to pause your top ten ads for a week only to find that when you turn them back on they've lost their proverbial juice.)

3) **Time constraints**. Amazon ads don't have to be "nursed" on a daily basis. I do try to check my dashboard at least a couple times a week, but that's often just a glance. If a new ad is losing me a lot of money, I pause it. Otherwise I tend to let things run. I'll analyze each individual ad, calculate my ROI, etc. a few times a month and otherwise let my ads work for me in the background.

Some people would rather be more hands-on all the time, especially when they're first starting out. So if you want to keep a very close eye on your ads (checking your stats every day, adjusting bids regularly, etc.), and you know you're going to be out of town, tied up writing a first draft, etc., you might want to schedule your ads to end on a certain date so you don't have to worry about them. If that's the case, however, I suggest you just pause them all and restart them once you're ready to get back into regular analysis (keeping in mind our unspoken rule of thumb mentioned above).

In other words, you probably don't need to adjust the start and end dates of your ads all that often.

Takeaways to Remember:

- Include the name and targeting options for your ad in its title. This will help you compile and analyze your data later.

- Use portfolios to organize your ads by series and/or to set a budget cap.

- You can set a low daily budget if you want, but even if you set a high one, it's unlikely that Amazon is going to spend all your money.

- Use the start and end date options however works best with your advertising plans and schedule, but don't spend a ton of time stressing out about either.

- When you find ads that work well, the best wisdom is to not tweak them too much or you might break something in the algorithm.

Automatic Targeting

Amazon's algorithm is pretty famous by now, especially in the author community. The algorithm is what decides if your book will appear as an also-bought beneath a wildly popular author in your genre. The algorithm is what decides if your title will be included in one of Amazon's daily emails it sends to its readers.

Amazon's algorithm is also what determines where your ad appears if you select the automatic targeting option for your sponsored ad.

The good news? Amazon's algorithm is really smart. That's why you don't often see vegan cookbooks advertised as sponsored products beneath Dan Brown's newest release.

I mentioned before that when I use auto targeting for my ads, my conversion rate (the ratio of reader clicks to actual sales I make) is really strong. In the past 30 days, I've spent $2771.38 on Amazon ads, gaining me 5,658 clicks and a total of 943 sales that Amazon considers a direct result of my ads. That means that on average this month, it takes me six clicks to get one sale. Not bad at all!

But those numbers change when I filter my results to include only my auto-targeted ads. Now, I have 1,237 clicks and 217 direct sales as a result of those clicks, meaning I only need 5.7 clicks to get a sale.

For math haters, out there, I'll give you the bottom. Auto-targeted ads aren't just easy to set up. They're also highly powerful at converting clicks into sales. The reason is that Amazon algorithm we talked about. Using its formulas and AI, Amazon knows exactly what kind of readers to show my book to.

There is only one real downside to auto-targeted ads. If your book isn't getting many (or any) sales right now, Amazon's algorithm might not know where to place it. So if you're brand-new to publishing or trying to promote a book that hasn't sold many copies recently, your ad might not ever "turn on" (meaning Amazon might not start showing it to readers). The good news is you aren't losing money (because your ad isn't getting any clicks), but the bad news is your ad isn't earning you extra royalties either.

If you fall into the "no-or-few-sales" camp, you can still set up your auto-targeted ad without risk. It just might not take off, and all you will have lost is about thirty seconds of your time.

Because auto ads rely on all the metadata you give when you set up your book, make sure your keywords and selected categories are on spot. Don't put your steamy romance into a clean and wholesome category because you think it'll be easier to rank. You want to give Amazon the best data so when you set up your auto ads they know exactly who will like to read your specific title.

Here's how you can set up your own auto-targeted ads:

1) After you've filled in your title, budget, and start and end dates, select the button that says "automatic targeting."

2) Under campaign bidding strategy, select "Dynamic bids – down only." This means you're giving Amazon permission to lower your bid when it saves you money but you aren't giving them permission to increase your bid. In general, sticking with dynamic bids – down only means you get the most effective use of your advertising funds, and it's what I recommend for any type of ad you create.

3) Next, you'll get to select your ad format. This is when you decide whether you want to add text with your ad or run an ad with simply your book cover, title, etc. Let's take just a couple minutes to discuss the differences of both options.

Custom text vs standard ads. If you select custom text, that allows you to add a short blurb about your book. Amazon has a few restrictions about the kinds of things you can say (don't call yourself a bestseller or compare yourself to another author). Custom text can be a decent way to tell readers a bit about your book before they click, but here are all the reasons why I choose standard ads and run my campaigns with no text.

First of all, in all the tests I've created, text ads never performed better than my standard (textless) ads. So I have data to show that standard ads give the same or sometimes better results when it comes to clicks and sales.

Secondly, standard ads are significantly easier to set up and manage. You don't have to think up a new tagline each time you advertise your book or test different versions of different hooks to see what works best.

Another reason I prefer to run ads with no text is for the reader experience. I want a reader to see my book cover in an ad and immediately click to my sales page. I don't want them to slow down and read my little blurb and then decide if it's a book they'd like. I want to get them to the sales page as quickly as I can, then let the sales page do the job of selling my book.

For all these reasons, I recommend choosing standard ads. Doing ads with text probably won't hurt you per se, but they'll take more time and you may not get the best results. If you're just looking for me to tell you exactly what to do, go ahead and select the standard ad box.

Advertising a single book or entire series. If you choose a standard ad, you have the option to advertise an entire series at once, not just a single book.

Some authors only advertise book one in a series, and that's totally your choice. The idea here is that people will start with book one, so may as well not "waste" clicks going to other books.

In my experience, I prefer to run ads to an entire series at once for multiple reasons. First of all, it's very easy. I can just add all the books in my series to one ad and it only takes me an extra two or three seconds more than it would to advertise a single title.

Advertising an entire series in this way saves you a lot of time and is great for brand awareness. Remember, you aren't paying for people to see your ad. They're only paying when somebody clicks your ad. If you get several books in the same series advertised on the same page, it's great for brand awareness, and it makes your series look a lot more popular than a solo ad would.

Ad groups. If you make a standard ad, you'll be prompted to name your ad group, which is the group of books you'll be promoting. Even if you're just advertising one book, they'll ask you to name your ad group. I just stick with their default, which is why every single ad group in my dashboard is named ad group. You don't have to put a lot of time or thought into that side of things.

4) Choose the book(s) you want to promote. This book must be one you've published through your KDP dashboard. You can select all the books in your series as a nice way to save time. Most of the ads I run are promoting the entire series. Although some writers choose to only advertise one book, I've never lost money advertising an entire series, and I love the extra brand awareness it brings, so the ads I create promote a whole series. I even throw the box sets in the same ad as well to save time and effort.

4) Enter your bid. If you're new to Amazon ads, pick a number between 60-100% of the default bid Amazon suggests. (We will go into more details about bidding later. For now, we're just figuring out the nuts and bolts of getting an ad started.) You can ignore the button about setting bids by group. Amazon gives you quite a few more bells and whistles than you actually need, and this is one of those things that you just don't need to worry about.

5) Negative targeting is where you can select if there are any products or keywords that you don't want Amazon to use. Some examples of negative keywords you might choose to add might be "audiobook," "paperback," or "kindle unlimited" if your books aren't in those formats, but in general you can trust Amazon's algorithm to figure this out on their own. (They probably won't show your ad to somebody searching for "cowboy romance paperback" if they know your book is only available in Kindle.)

I generally ignore negative targeting. The one time when it can be useful is if you're an author who writes in different genres under the same name. For example, if Katie writes romance and suspense, when she runs ads for suspense, she might put "romance" as a negative keyword so that readers searching for her books in one genre don't see ads for her other genres.

5) Click launch. Your campaign will be reviewed and can start generating impressions, clicks, and (hopefully) sales within a few hours! Easy peasy, right?

The Ad Review Process

When you launch your ad, you'll get an email that your ad's been moderated. This just means it's being reviewed. If you set up lots of ads like I do, you can create a filter if you use gmail to automatically delete these emails so your inbox doesn't get run over. You'll also get an email to tell you if your ad has been accepted or rejected.

Amazon has some pretty strict guidelines about what they do and don't allow to pass their review screening process. The good news is even if your ad is rejected, Amazon will create a copy of that ad, put it in your drafts folder, and you can change it to meet their standards.

Here are a few tips if you want to ensure your ads are accepted, especially if you do choose to write text to go with your ad:

1) **Watch out for typos.** Amazon really does check on this and will reject ads with misspelled words or grammar mistakes.

2) **Use correct punctuation** and avoid extra exclamation marks. Also avoid WRITING WORDS IN ALL CAPS to draw attention to your copy. This will get your ad rejected.

3) **Avoid certain words.** You're likely to get your ad rejected if you call your book a bestseller or award-winner. You also can't say you're "better than" a certain author or series, although sometimes you can get by with something like "Fans of (author A) love these novels."

4) **Don't mention stars, price, or reviews**. Because your star rating can change over time, you aren't allowed to call your book 5-stars or anything like that. You also aren't supposed to mention your book's price or any discounts, since these can change at any time. Same thing with quoting an Amazon review. Based on my experience, Amazon will reject nearly anything you put in quotes.

5) **Forbidden covers.** If you have a gun on your cover, it can't be pointing straight at the reader. Additionally, Amazon says it doesn't like sexually suggestive cover images (although plenty of these do seem to pass their review screening). If your ad gets rejected for a suggestive cover or title, you can always try resubmitting a similar ad in a few weeks, and often that's enough to get at least some of your ads approved.

6) **Miscellaneous forbidden content.** You aren't allowed to run ads for books that deal with drugs, illicit substances, harm to children/minors, or hate speech. Amazon also has a few restrictions on religious books. For example, if your book is about Religion A, you can't target a sacred text from Religion B. You can only target other books written for a Religion A audience. Although some of my friends in the Christian author space were worried about these restrictions, I've not heard of ads getting rejected for religious content.

If all this sounds like a lot to remember, don't worry about it too much. Amazon will tell you if your ad is rejected, and they will usually at least give you some clue as to why. They'll also set your ad in drafts, as I've mentioned, so you can edit and resubmit.

Takeaways to Remember:

- Automatic targeting is the easiest form of sponsored ad to create and also one of the most effective because it relies on Amazon's AI to find just the right targets for your book.

- If your book hasn't sold many copies yet, Amazon might not have enough data to know where to run it so your ad might not take off. You won't lose any money, but your book will just sit there doing nothing. The good news is you can go on to some of the other ad options we'll talk about next, and once you get more sales, your auto ads may take off too.

- You can run ads with or without text. If you choose the option to run your ads without text, you can advertise an entire series at once, which is how I advertise the bulk of my books.

- There are a few things that will get your ads rejected. It's important to have a passing familiarity with Amazon's advertising policies.

Using Keyword Targeting with Your Ads

Now that you've seen how simple it can be to set up your ads with automatic targeting, we can start playing around with some of Amazon's keyword options.

Just like before, let's start with the easiest of options and move up from there.

Amazon's Suggested Keywords

First, let's talk about making use of the keywords Amazon will suggest for you. The first thing you want to do is create a new sponsored ad. Give it a name that includes its title as well as something like "suggested keywords" because we'll be talking first about how to use the keywords that Amazon is going to suggest for your book.

After you've set your daily budget, select the option for manual targeting (not automatic). You'll keep on choosing "dynamic bids – down only" like before and pick the book(s) you want to advertise. Next Amazon will ask if you want to target by keyword or by product. For this chapter, our focus will be on keyword ads.

(Quick note: if you'd like to see these ads created in real time, you can watch the videos in my Amazon Ads Starter Kit which is free with the purchase of this book! Just visithttp://courses.alanaterry.com/kit for access.)

Next we'll set our default bid. Just as before, I suggest you set your default bid to somewhere between 60-100% of Amazon's suggested bid. You also have the option to filter your keywords based on broad, phrase, or exact wording. To keep this super simple and the most effective, just keep all these options selected. This means that you'll still get clicks even if somebody doesn't type in the EXACT word you did. For example, if you type in mysteries (plural) somebody who searches for mystery (singular) can still find your book since you've selected broad and phrase and exact wording.

Next you'll see a list of suggested keywords. Some of these will make a ton of sense. When I select my women's fiction novel *Beauty from Ashes*, the first few suggested keywords that come up are my name, the names of some of my most popular books and series, and some genre keywords like "Christian fiction".

When you see a keyword that makes sense for your particular book, click add. You may also find some keywords that make very little sense at all, or perhaps are so broad you don't want to select them. For example, some of the suggested keywords that come up for *Beauty from Ashes* are "women" and "novel," both of which are so broad I decided not to use them. In general, I've found that it's more effective to run ads using fewer, more specific keywords. And yes, I've practiced doing it the other way too, with hundreds of ads with up to a thousand keywords each, and it turned into more trouble than it was worth cutting out keywords that didn't belong.

That's why my recommendation is to run ads with a few keywords (like a couple dozen or fewer) that make perfect sense for your readers rather than casting a huge net with tons of random words you'll just have to sift through later.

After you've added whichever suggested keywords make sense for you and your particular book, you'll see a spot where you can select negative keywords. These are words that you DON'T want Amazon to use to target your book. Like we mentioned before, you don't need to spend tons of time worrying about negative keywords (most of my ads don't have any negative keywords listed), but here are some situations where you might choose to use negative keywords.

1) **To avoid confusion**. Let's say you're running ads for your thriller called *Putting Them Down*. You want to use your book's title as one of your keywords, but there also is a self-help book by a famous veterinarian by that same name. Dr. Smiles's book helps people cope with the loss of their family pet. In this case, you can set keywords to exclude like "pet" and "Dr. Smiles" so when people are searching specifically for Dr. Smiles's book, your thriller book won't appear as a sponsored product in those searches.

2) **To get more genre-specific**. If you write clean and wholesome novels and are using broad keywords like "romance," you might decide to exclude words like "erotic" and "steamy" to further specify your niche.

3) If you write in a heavily KU-dominated niche and your book is NOT in KU, you can set parameters to exclude "Kindle Unlimited" as a search keyword.

That way if people are looking for a KU read specifically, they won't waste your money by clicking on your ad only to decide it isn't the right format for them.

4) Another keyword you might want to exclude is "free," since you want to attract readers ready and willing to pay money for your novels.

Please DO NOT do what some authors do and put your own name in the negative targeting list. You want to make it as easy as possible for people who are searching for your books to find you, and you don't want them to get distracted by somebody else's ad and never landing on your book page at all.

Once you have your suggested keywords selected and have added any negative keywords you want to exclude, you're ready to launch your ad!

Takeaways to Remember:

- When you select manual targeting, Amazon will give you a list of keywords they suggest you use for that particular book.
- You may want to exclude search keywords that are too generic (like "book" or "novel").
- You can exclude certain keywords like "free" to narrow down where you want your ads to appear.

Creating Genre Keywords

Now that you've seen how to target some of Amazon's suggested keywords, it's time to start making some of your own keyword lists! This is where you can have a lot of fun and get really creative. To use your own keywords, follow all the instructions from above where you were relying on Amazon's suggested keywords. This time, however, when you see the spot where Amazon lists out keywords they recommend, you can click the tab that says "Enter list" and add your own keywords.

It's really easy to get carried away here. I actually have a file on my computer with 100,000 keywords ready to use! But honestly, that list took me WAY too long to make, and my ads do better with more specific targeting anyway. Once you've gotten the hang of the ads dashboard, you also may choose to compile massive keyword lists like these, however I have ALWAYS had better results using a smaller number of specific keywords instead of hundreds of generic ones. Most of my keyword ads at the moment have fewer than fifty keywords.

One thing I do recommend doing is using Amazon's auto-predictor to help select your keywords. First, let's start with genre keywords. If this were my ad, I would name this one something like "Book1 – genre keywords." When you get to the location in the ad creation dashboard where you can enter your own keywords, type in your genre. You'll see that Amazon will pull up multiple other suggested phrases. Select any of these that apply. (Most of them will. The only ones that won't might be if a subgenre comes up that isn't a good fit for your book, or if a search term comes up like "audiobook" or "paperback" and your book isn't available in that particular format.)

You can see that this method hardly takes any more time than relying on Amazon's suggested keywords and can be just as effective. Select whichever genre keywords make sense for your book, and you've got another ad ready to run!

Quick note: Amazon will allow you to select up to 1,000 keywords for an individual ad, but don't feel like you've got to add anywhere close to that many. The bulk of ads I have running now have 10-30 keywords in each. This actually makes it easier for me to know which kind of keywords work the best instead of having to sift through thousands and thousands of keywords for data.

You'll notice when you add your keywords that you have different options here for bidding. In general, the easiest option is to create a default bid that will be the same for each keyword you create. Keep each match type selected (broad, phrase, and exact), and in general don't bid too high until you've got some experience under your belt. For now, I suggest you stick with bids that are about 60% - 100% of what Amazon suggests.

Takeaways to Remember:

- To add your own keywords, select manual targeting, keyword targeting, then find the tab that says "enter list."

- Using Amazon's auto-prediction tool will help you come up with keywords that are a good fit for your book.

- You can add up to 1,000 keywords per ad, however this isn't necessary or even recommended. Having ten really targeted keywords is a lot better than 500 generic ones.

- You have the choice to adjust your bids based on each individual keyword. But, for now, it's easiest to keep things simple and rely on a default bid that matches or is a little lower than what Amazon suggests.

Creating Author Keywords

Now you've seen how to add your own keywords and how Amazon will help you fill your keywords with search terms they know people are using. I think it's time for a short recap. If you're following the instructions in this book step by step, you've now created three different sponsored product ads using three different targeting methods:

1) automatic targeting

2) manual targeting and Amazon's suggested keywords

3) manual targeting and genre keywords

If you're launching a new book and want to run ads but are short on time, these three ads can get you pretty far. But there are many other targeting options that are worth talking about.

The next type of ads we'll discuss are ads that target a specific author by name. Let me tell you about some mistakes I made that you can avoid. I used to be insanely vigilant about setting up these keyword lists. I would find and manually add every single book title that a particular author wrote, and I even signed up to follow nearly a hundred authors on Amazon so I could update my lists when a new novel came out.

In short, I spent a lot of unnecessary time!

Here's what I do now when I want to target Author A:

1) Name my ad "Book X – Author A."

2) Go through the steps outlined above to set up manual targeting by keyword.

3) Type Author A's name in where it says "enter list" and select all the search terms that come up.

4) Launch my ad.

Sometimes if you're targeting a lesser-known author (which is a great idea since these clicks are less competitive and therefore cheaper), Amazon might not have many keywords that come up as suggested uses. If that's the case, or if you simply don't feel like creating individual ads targeting individual authors, you can add several authors to your keywords list following the directions above. Name your ad something like "Book X – multiple authors," and you're set to launch. Having 3-5 authors as keywords in one ad is a really nice way to set things up without spending tons of extra time.

Even though you might like the idea of targeting as many authors as possible, you'll get the best results (and endear yourself to the Amazon algorithm) when you focus on authors who write in your specific sub-genre or sub-niche. A really quick way to gauge if another author would make a good target is to go to their Amazon page and take a look at their book covers. Would your covers fit in with what you see? If so, they're probably a good match. Remember, for Amazon ads, readers are making split-second decisions based mostly off your cover, so find others that look like yours and these will make good targets.

Here are some more ideas for finding author names to target:

1) Poll your readers and ask who their favorite authors are, and select the names that come up most.

2) Go to your Amazon author page and see what authors show up in the sidebar under "Customers Also Bought Items By."

3) Sign up to get emails from Bookbub about books in your genre and target authors who seem to be a good match.

There aren't any real "rules" about whether you should target authors with fewer readers or more readers than you. The only thing to keep in mind is that it's best to find a few authors who are very similar to you than to find hundreds of authors that are kind of like you. And also remember that really famous authors will be more competitive as keywords, so your cost per click might increase. For that reason, some authors like focusing primarily on targeting midlist authors.

Some advertisers feel bad targeting other writers. It can feel as if you're trying to "steal" readers from someone else. There's no reason to feel this way, but if it becomes a big roadblock, here are a few things you can try.

1) Stick with targeting genre keywords. This isn't highly recommended, however, as targeting by an author name will usually get you cheaper clicks and better results than targeting by genre.

2) You might decide not to target authors you personally know, but I don't think this is a necessary step. Especially if your writing friend isn't running their own Amazon ads, you may as well use their name for your keywords. Like I said earlier, sponsored ads aren't going anywhere, and I assume your friend would rather see your books on their sales page than a stranger's.

3) Shift your mindset. Out of all the possible options, this is the one I favor the most. Remember that there are enough readers for everyone out there, and you getting a book sale doesn't mean you're stealing money out of another author's bank account. Stop looking at other authors in your genre as your competition and remember that the more quality books get out there and succeed, the more demand there will be for even more high-quality books in your genre.

Takeaways to Remember:

- You don't need to spend a ton of time compiling the names of every single book or series an author has created. Just let Amazon's predictive text tool do the work for you.

- Try using 3-5 author names as your keywords for each ad, and make sure you're sticking closely to your subgenre.

Creating Your Own Keywords

If you've been following along and created the ads we've already mentioned in this book, you'll have created about 95% of the sponsored ads I currently run for my books. My sponsored product ads are a mix of auto-targeting, suggested keyword targeting, and creating quick and easy lists of genre and author keywords.

I should mention here that targeting YOURSELF as an author is a great marketing strategy. It is good for brand recognition as well as for flat-out book sales if your books are the sponsored ads on your own page. Unfortunately, there are some authors who HATE the thought of paying for clicks for themselves. The idea goes like this: *If somebody searches for my name, they're looking for a book by me. So that means I'm already going to get that sale, so why would I PAY Amazon to get them to find my books?*

Well, by targeting yourself you're making it easier for your most loyal readers to find you. That's good. You don't want your biggest fan to type your name into the search bar and have to scroll down five different books until they see one of yours. Otherwise you'll risk them seeing somebody else's ad, getting distracted, and never making it to your sales page at all.

There's also the straight up data that supports targeting yourself. The ads that I run targeting myself have a significantly better conversion rate than my other kind of ads. I said before that it takes on average six clicks on my ad for a reader to choose to buy one of my books. For ads that I target to myself and my own books, it only takes four clicks!

(This is also a great reminder of why it's important to name your ads based on targeting. To figure out my conversion rate above, all I had to do was search all the ads that had my last name in the title.)

Now that you know how to set up manual keyword ads, you can take that info and run with it. In fact, 99% of the sponsored ads I have currently running are set up using the methods we've already discussed. However, I know some authors really enjoy creating vast piles of keywords (remember that 100,000 list I mentioned?), so I'll mention a few places where you can do more research to get more keywords to test.

1) **Publisher Rocket (formerly KDP Rocket)**. This is a paid software where you can type in a genre, author name, or book title, and get a list of keywords based on what people are currently searching for on Amazon. It's quick, easy, and if your goal is to create large lists of keywords with very little work, it's worth the money.

2) **Bookbub**. For a while, I ran an ad targeting only books that had been featured recently on Bookbub. Since you know these books are going to have lots of visibility (at least for a short period of time), it makes sense to want your books to appear on their sales pages.

3) **Browse Amazon**. You can compile all kinds of keyword lists from Amazon itself. Browse for the most popular books or authors in your genre. Create a keyword list of books about to come out or that have just been released. Make a list of all your also-boughts or lists of all the also-boughts

by another popular author in your genre. The possibilities here are basically endless.

4) **Get a data scraper**. There are tools that will actually crawl across webpages and compile all the data they find into easy spreadsheets. The one I used to rely on is a free chrome extension called Instant Data Scraper. Once you have it downloaded on your browser, you can go to Amazon's bestseller page and have it compile that list into a spreadsheet for you.

Unfortunately, data scrapers aren't super user-friendly, and I'm not savvy enough to always get mine working properly. It was a useful tool for me to compile that massive keyword list, but I don't rely on that anymore anyway, and it's definitely not a necessary step.

That should give you some ideas on how to compile your own keyword lists, but please keep in mind you certainly don't have to follow any of these steps. I found that having hundreds of thousands of keywords was really time consuming (not to mention overwhelming). Also, you can end up with lots of keywords that aren't a good fit for your book or are too broad to work well for you. In my experience, shorter and more specific keyword lists work better and are far easier to create, analyze, and maintain.

Takeaways to Remember:

- You should definitely target yourself in your ads.

- You can use all kinds of methods to compile massive keyword lists, but it can be time-consuming and isn't at all necessary.

- In general, smaller and more specific keyword lists are more likely to perform better than massive lists compiled using the methods above.

Targeting Specific Products

Let's do a quick recap that includes a small(ish) vocab lesson.

When you create your sponsored ads, you have three main options. You can create auto ads (discussed two chapters ago). You can create keyword ads (discussed in the last chapter). And you can create product ads, which is what we're discussing now. Product targeting, like it sounds, involves targeting specific products or sales categories, not just keywords.

There are two types of product ads to explore. Category ads let you target an entire genre. Individual product ads let you target by ASIN.

Let's talk first about category ads, which are very easy and one of the least time-intensive kinds of ads to set up.

To set up an ad that targets certain genres or categories:

1) Create a sponsored ad. Select the manual targeting option, then select the product targeting option. (Other options like your bidding strategy and decisions like whether you use text or not will stay the same no matter what type of ad you're making. If you need a refresher, choose "dynamic bids – down only," "standard ad" for no text, and choose a bid between 60% - 100% of what Amazon suggests.)

2) If Amazon has a suggested category for your book, you'll see it listed. Select that option and run your ad.

If Amazon recommends multiple categories you have a few options, and they're all worth playing around with. You can target just one category at a time and see how it does if you love data collecting. However, if you just want to save time and do what's easiest, it's also totally acceptable to add several genres to your category ads, just as long as they match your genre well.

You may see that Amazon gives some refining options where you can only show your ad on products that have a certain number of stars, etc. You're welcome to play around with these settings but they're not all that important.

Category ads can be really effective, but they do come with a few potential drawbacks that are worth noting. First off, your book might not fall into one of Amazon's recommended categories. This has historically been a problem for Christian fiction authors like me, since the option for specific sub-genres in the category offerings are quite limited. Unless you're in a very broad genre, you may run into similar problems as well, which is why you may choose to focus on targeting individual products instead of broad genre categories.

Secondly, category ads can sometimes be costly. The clicks are more expensive on average than some of the other types of ads we've mentioned. This is because lots of authors, for example, will advertise their books in the historical fiction category. Not as many authors, by contrast, will advertise using a keyword like "ancient Greek historical romance." A rule of thumb to keep in mind with Amazon ads is that the broader your targeting is, the more you will likely pay and the fewer sales you might make. For cheapest clicks and highest sales conversion, stick with more specific targeting methods. If your goal, however, is brand awareness, category ads are some of the best options for getting a lot of exposure to a lot of readers.

Targeting Individual Products

When you set up product targeting, you can create two types of ads, category ads like what we just talked about, and individual product ads, which are the most specific type of ad you can make.

Categories, as I just mentioned, can work well in certain genres, but there aren't that many options if you're writing for niche markets. In these cases, you'll probably find better results when you target individual products instead. This is how to tell Amazon exactly which book sales pages you want your ads to show on.

When you tell Amazon to target individual products, they'll give you one of three choices.

1) **Suggested.** If Amazon has recommendations for products to target, you may find them here. You can choose to add any or all of these that you feel are good fits for your book.

2) **Search.** Technically, you can use this function to search for one author and select all their books, however the search option doesn't seem to work as well as it should, and many times you'll notice many books are missing. Hopefully it's a bug that Amazon will eventually fix, since being able to search for one author and target all their individual books would be a great tool.

3) **Enter list**. This is what I use most when I create individual product ads. This allows you to copy and paste a list of ASIN numbers into the ads dashboard and have your ads show up on those sales pages.

What's an ASIN? It's basically the Amazon equivalent of a barcode number or ISBN. To find a book's ASIN, just go to that specific page on Amazon, and the ASIN will be right there in the webpage. For example, if your book's URL is amazon.com/gp/product/B07P7PM642, the ASIN is the ten numbers and digits (in this case B07P7PM642)

I recommend you compile a list of all your own ASIN numbers and enter these into your ads. That way you're not only targeting your own name as a keyword like we mentioned before, but you're also targeting all your own specific books.

I also recommend you go through this process to target specific books by other authors. Finding products to target is very similar to the methods outlined above in compiling keywords. You can target books on the Amazon bestseller lists, the hot new releases in your genre, Bookbub featured deals ... basically the possibilities are endless. Just remember that even though your first inclination might be to run out and find hundreds or thousands of products to target, you really don't have to get that specific.

There is one free tool that can help you compile lots of ASINs right from Amazon without having to copy and paste from the URL. The tool is called the ASIN picker. You can search for it as a free chrome extension. Then when you're in your browser browsing the Amazon Kindle store, you can click on any book you want and it will save the ASIN in a file you can copy and paste to create your ad.

Publisher Rocket also has a tool to allow you to copy and paste ASINs of other books related to yours that can be good targets.

Takeaways to Remember:

- Targeting by category is quick and easy but may not work well if your specific sub-genre isn't one of the possible choices.

- Keep a list of all your own ASINs and upload these so you're targeting your own books.

- Use the ASIN Picker chrome extension tool for an easy way to grab a lot of ASINs at once.

Non-Sponsored Ads

Congratulations! We've covered all the different types of sponsored product ads available to create on Amazon. We talked about auto ads, keyword ads, and the two types of product ads (category and individual products).

You now have all the information you need to create any type of sponsored product ad you want! Then you can take that information to set up other types of Amazon ads too, since the targeting options for these ads will follow the same basic premises that we already discussed. Similarly, the analysis and data we'll be discussing in the next session applies regardless of what type of ad you're running.

In other words, now that you know how to set up sponsored ads, you can apply the exact same principles to lockscreen ads, headline ads, etc. You can also start to experiment with ads in other countries. If your book is in English, I recommend adding Canada, UK and Australia first. To run your Amazon ads in other countries, just log onto your KDP account, click the marketing tab, and choose whichever Amazon store you want to set up ads in. The setup will be the same (or quite similar) to what we've talked about before. Just be careful to remember that your bids will be in the currency of that country, so do the mental conversion, and keep in mind that some credit cards or debit cards will charge you a nominal transaction fee for international payments.

Before we talk about analyzing your ads, I want to commend you for your progress thus far. You're a busy writer who would probably rather be working on your next masterpiece than reading (or listening to) a book about Amazon ads. But you're here. You're investing in your business, which puts you well on your way to more and more success.

By now, I hope you've come to realize a few things:

1) Creating your ads doesn't have to be all that time consuming.

2) While you definitely COULD spend hours of your life compiling thousands of possible targets, you certainly don't have to. The most effective ads are almost always going to be the ones that are fairly simple, specific, and quick to create.

3) Targeting yourself is always a good idea.

4) Amazon ads can be FUN, and Amazon ads can change the trajectory of your entire career.

When I first was learning ads, my husband worked as a bivocational pastor, meaning that in addition to his duties at our church, he had to work a second job so we could make ends meet. After I started ads in 2017, he was able to give up that second job. In 2020, I was able to take a fiction sabbatical and still end up with more profit from my book sales than any previous year. A year later, we moved our family into our dream home. So I'm not exaggerating when I tell you that Amazon ads changed my life.

Growing up, I was the shyest kid at my entire high school. I guarantee you that nobody who knew me back then would be surprised AT ALL to hear that I'm a stay-at-home homeschooling mom.

What WOULD surprise them is that I'm also something of a kick-butt marketing ninja. To me, tossing money into ads and seeing that money double year after year is like an addictive smartphone game. I get a serious dopamine kick opening up my KDP dashboard to check my sales stats. I say all this to tell you that even if you don't think you have a marketing bone in your entire body, running ads can actually be fun.

Yes, I said it. Fun.

The other day, I was tired. I've made myself a promise to take a week off a quarter, and since we were getting close to the end of the month, I knew I had a lot of work to accomplish so I could take that time off. I had a novel that really needed to be edited. You know what I did instead?

I poured myself a cup of coffee, put on my favorite fuzzy bathrobe, and sat in our downstairs recliner calculating my monthly revenue from ads.

Think I'm crazy? I know for a fact I'm not the only author who finds running ads fun, addictive, and even relaxing. When our family is watching a movie and I want to be with them while still feeling somewhat productive, I'll pull out my laptop and create some Amazon ads while we watch. When my husband runs into the store and I'm in the car for ten minutes with nothing better to do, I pull up my ads dashboard on my phone and adjust bids as necessary.

What I'm getting at is that as an author, you don't need to think of ads as just some massive have-to. Once you get your feet wet, once you see those first few sales coming in ... you just might realize they're an awful lot of fun.

Takeaways to Remember:

- This book focused on teaching you how to set up sponsored product ads, but now that you know the basics of targeting you'll be able to set up other types of ads and market your books in other countries.

- To have the most success with your ads, you need to keep track of your numbers as we'll talk about in the next few chapters, but that doesn't necessarily have to be a bore.

Data and Analysis

This is the section so many authors dread because it has to do with numbers. But you know what? You don't have to be a math geek or a numbers guru to get helpful tips out of this chapter. You're talking with the woman who has a deadly allergy to Excel, formulas, and spreadsheets of all kinds. But you're also talking with the woman who just admitted that when I'm stressed out and want to chillax, I do my ads calculations.

Did I mention I do a big chunk of these by hand? I find it ridiculously and inexplicably therapeutic. But don't worry. The numbers we'll be discussing today are the same whether you're using spreadsheets, calculators, online tracking tools, or old-fashioned paper and pencil.

First of all, let's talk about a few key phrases so we're all on the same page. And in case my previous mentions of numbers have given you flashbacks to high-school math class, don't worry. None of this will be on the test. In fact, now that you know how to set up your ads, you could skip this section entirely. The problem is that setting up your ads is only the first half of the ads game. The second half is tracking your ads and making adjustments as necessary.

This doesn't need to be a grueling, time-consuming chore that sucks joy out of your life ten hours a day. Nobody's going to force you to wear pocket protectors and sit in a cubicle like some unhappy junior accountant. (No offense if junior accounting is your thing. I just know it certainly isn't mine!)

The point I'm trying to make is that analyzing your ads is important work but it can be done on the go. I have my ads dashboard bookmarked on my smartphone. If I'm watching my kids bounce around at the trampoline park (like I was when I wrote the first edition of this book), sitting in a theater before a movie starts (or waiting to see if there's one more Marvel post-credit scene), or killing time at a doctor's office waiting room, I can easily pull up my dashboard and check in with my ads. It's not something that takes *extra* time out of my day, and it doesn't have to take extra time out of yours either.

Terms You Should Know

Some of these terms you'll already know, but let's be sure to cover the bases anyway. We'll keep it brief, keep it snappy, and then we can move on to where the good stuff really happens.

Here are some of the terms you should know when running ads for your book:

1) **Profit:** It's what we all want in this business, right? (That and an entire army of fans eagerly waiting to buy and devour our books before leaving glowing five-star reviews.) Your profit is simply the amount of money you make minus the amount of money you spend.

A positive profit means you're making more money than you spend. A negative profit means you're spending more money than you're making.

For example, say you spend $25 on ads for a book and earn $75 in royalties. Congratulations. You've earned $50 in profit.

Your profit may also be negative. If you spend $25 on ads for a book and earn $20 in royalties, your profit is negative $5. In other words, you've lost $5 on that ad.

A quick word on profit. Profit is the bottom line. It's what you get to take home at the end of the day. It's the money you have in the bank to pay yourself, your mortgage, your taxes, etc. I started my first Amazon ad in August of 2017, and by fall of the next year, my income bumped up to over $10,000 in book sales a month. That didn't mean, however, that I was $10,000 a month richer. First of all, I was putting nearly half of the income I made back into ads. I did this for a year or so in order to scale up my ads as quickly as possible without going into debt.

Bottom line? It's fun to talk numbers. It's fun to look at the past twelve months and realize you're now an official six-figure author. But at the end of the day, the number that really matters is profit.

2) **ROI (Return on Investment):** Your ROI is a number indicating if your ad is profitable and by how much. The calculation for ROI is simple. Take your total profit and divide that by how much money you spent on ads. The higher your ROI percentage, the better your ad is doing.

A while back I had a Bookbub featured deal. I spent $480 to have my Christian fiction novel promoted to Bookbub's readers. On my promo day, I earned about $510 in book sales for that particular book.

My profit was $30. My ROI was $30 divided by $480, or 6.25%. If this were my only profit, I wouldn't be all that thrilled. However, that is only the income earned for the one day of that ad and doesn't account for the additional sales I received from the added exposure or the sales I made on the rest of the books in that series. Which brings me to our next definition.

3) **Read-Through:** If you write books in a series, whether fiction or nonfiction, your read-through is one of the most important numbers to keep track of. Your read-through number is a reflection of how many follow-up sales you make in your entire series as a result of one sale of book one.

Let me share some of my own numbers as an example. One of my most popular series (right now at least) is a nine-book Christian suspense series. The series itself is chronological, meaning readers start with book one and move down the list until they reach book nine.

Based on trends that I track on an ongoing basis, I know that over 40% of readers who buy book one will go on to buy book two. I also have numbers to track what percentage of readers go on to buy books three, four, five, and so on. By the time a reader has made it to book five, my read-through rates for the rest of the series are pretty consistently in the 90% range or higher, meaning that if a reader gets to book five, they're almost guaranteed to buy the rest of the books.

These numbers tell me two important things. First, they tell me trends in readership. If, for example, I look at my series and find that my read-through rate between books three and four has dropped significantly, that could mean I did something in book three that made my readers mad. If you kill off the beloved pet dog in book six, don't be surprised when your read-through numbers drop significantly when it comes to book seven!

Even more importantly than tracking percentages is calculating your read-through value, which is the amount of income your series will generate for every sale of book one. When it comes to running ads, knowing your read-through value is important because it allows you to calculate how much money you can afford to spend in order to sell one copy of book one in your series.

Remember that Bookbub featured deal I just mentioned? Sometimes I've managed to lose money on a Bookbub deal, but in the end, it's still worked out for me. Early in my writing career, I published a short romance series, veering away from suspense for a bit. I was thrilled when I got a Bookbub featured deal for the first book in that series, but my results were underwhelming, to say the least. I paid Bookbub $480 and only made about $440 in sales royalties for the day of my featured deal. In other words, I lost $40 and had a negative ROI.

However, lots of people who read book one in that series went on to buy the other three books. During the month of my Bookbub featured deal, the series overall earned around $950. Because of read-through, my profit was back in the black and my ROI was over 100% (meaning I more than doubled the money I spent for that Bookbub deal).

Some authors turn off their Amazon ads because in the dashboard it looks like they're losing money, but when you account for readthrough they're actually making a killing. I have one series that brings in over $12 for every sale I make of book one. With this number in mind, I don't mind losing some money up front if it means more sales in the future.

For example, right now in my Amazon ads dashboard, I can see that I've spent about $1200 on ads for book one this month. That ad reported 236 copies sold, which means I've earned about $660 in sales. Bottom line here looks like I lost nearly half my ad spend. The good news is that for every sale of book one, I know I will earn on average more than $12 in sales from the entire series as readers make their way through my catalog.

To estimate my actual profit from these ads, I can take the 236 copies of book one I sold, multiply that number by $12 (the amount I know I get on average every time I get one new reader), and now I can estimate over $2,800 in projected sales, which is more than double what I spent on ads.

Make it simple for me, please! There's a chance I lost a reader or two right here, so let me give you the absolute bottom line. If you HATE looking at numbers and want the easiest way to know if your ads are profitable, you just need to look at two numbers. How much are you spending on your ads, and how much money is that specific book or series bringing in? To get the easiest, fastest, at-a-glance check-in with your profit, just look in your Amazon ads dashboard to see how much you spent. Then go to your KDP dashboard to see how much you earned from that book or series in the same amount of time.

Are you making more than you spent? Then you have a profit.

This is the simple version. There are pitfalls to it, and it can get complicated if you're advertising on multiple platforms or have a significant number of organic sales to account for, so this method isn't for everyone. But it IS for you if you want to know that you're profiting and you're ready to figure it out in the easiest, fastest way possible.

Bottom line for people who don't want to go into math? Look at your data for the past two weeks to one month. Have you earned more in book sales than you spent on Amazon ads? Then you're just fine.

Back to read-through. Some people will want to stop with the simple method, but for those of you ready to go one step deeper, let's talk about how to calculate your own read-through value.

First, find out how many ebook copies of book one you've sold in a given amount of time. (Only track the copies you've actually sold. If you're in KU, ignore income from page reads for this half of the calculation.)

Second, find out how much money you've earned from that entire series in the same amount of time. In this case, you want to include your Kindle Unlimited income if you're in KU as well as sales from your Amazon paperbacks.

Take the total amount you've earned from the series and divide by the number of ebook copies of book one you've sold. This is how much money you can expect to earn in your series for every ebook sale of book one.

Here's what this looks like practically. When I first launched three novels in an Alaskan-based Christian suspense series, I wanted to know how much I could spend on ads and still be profitable. So I went into my KDP sales dashboard. Book one had sold 321 copies, and I made $1,990 in sales from all three books.

To find my read-through value, I took the total number I've earned in that series ($1,990) and divided it by the number of copies of book one I've sold (321). The number I got is $6.20. This means that for every copy of book one I sold, I could expect to earn a little over $6 in sales from the entire series.

How did knowing that number practically impact my ability to run ads? Looking at my Amazon ads dashboard in the first month that series launched, I spent $909 on ads, sold 184 copies of book one, and earned $642 in book one royalties as a result of my ads. On the surface, it looks like I lost money and should have turned off these ads.

However, because I calculated my read-through value, I estimated that the 184 sales I made on book one would bring in over $1,100, meaning I had a net profit and a positive ROI, so I kept the ads going. Now that series has brought in well over $50,000 in book sales, and every dollar I put into running ads to it doubles my return.

As with most things statistical, the more data you have on your read-through sales, the more accurate your results will be. I suggest you calculate this number from no less than a month's worth of data. If your series has been published for a while, you can even calculate your read-through numbers over a given quarter. Just check in with your data every so often to make sure they're still accurate. Also, remember to take into account anything that might change your read-through rate. If you've recently run a 99-cent sale, changed prices or descriptions for your books, etc., these can and will impact your read-through rate. For your initial calculations, try to use data from months where you haven't changed anything up lately to get the best results.

How does read-through work for nonfiction authors? If you write nonfiction, you can still assume that readers who liked one of your books may go on to read another, even if those books aren't connected in a series. In this case, the readthrough discussion above can still prove helpful.

Similarly, if you use your writing to grow your platform, sell courses, attract coaching clients, etc., you can do a similar calculation to determine how much you should spend to advertise your book. Let's say in March you sold 100 books and had 10 people sign up to buy your $100 course because you linked to it at the end of your book. That means that for every book you sell, you can expect about $10 back from course sales. The formula here is to take all the money you earned from books AND courses, divided it by how many books you sold, and that will tell you on average how much you can spend on your ads to sell book one without losing money.

Takeaways to Remember:

- Profit is how much money you've earned minus how much you've spent. A negative profit means you've lost money. Positive profit means you've gained money.

- Return on investment (ROI) is your profit divided by how much you've spent. You want a positive ROI, the higher the percentage the better.

- If you write in a series, you should calculate your read-through value so you know how much money you'll likely earn for every copy you sell of book one.

- To calculate your read-through value the simplest way, take the total amount of earnings you've made for an entire series and divide it by the number of ebook sales you've made on book one. This will give you an estimate of how much money you'll make in the future for every sale of book one.

- The calculation for nonfiction authors selling courses or coaching is the amount you earned from book sales and associated course or coaching sales divided by how many copies of your book you sold in the same timeframe.

- Bottom line? Sometimes it will look in the Amazon ads dashboard like you're losing money, when you're actually making a very healthy profit once you account for other sales that came as a result of your ads.

Your Ads Dashboard

The Amazon ads dashboard has seen some tremendous upgrades and improvements since its original inception. When I first started teaching Amazon ads to authors, there was a significantly larger lag in sales reporting and anecdotal instances of under-reporting. There also weren't convenient ways to look at data over a specific time period, and KU authors just had to guess how much of their page read income came from Amazon ads.

In spite of all its improvements, the Amazon ads dashboard still has some limitations. If somebody clicks on an ad for one book then goes on to purchase a different book of yours, you'll be charged for that click but that sale won't count in your ads dashboard. When somebody sees your ad and borrows your book in KU, their page reads will show up in your dashboard for up to 14 days, after which any page reads won't be seen in your ads dashboard. That's why it's smart to also keep an eye on your actual sales reports in your KDP dashboard.

In my experience, the data I get from the ads dashboard is decently reliable enough that I use it to make decisions on which ads to pause, pull, or scale. Here are some of the metrics you can measure in your ads dashboard. The columns in your dashboard are customizable, so if you don't see a particular column in your default settings, you can click on the "columns" button and add the metrics you want to track.

1) **Spend**. This tells you how much money you've spent on any given ad. Remember, Amazon doesn't charge you for showing your ad to people. You only get charged when someone clicks. That basically means you're getting a lot of advertising for free!

2) **Impressions.** This is the number of people who have seen your ad. If your ad is active and Amazon is actively promoting it, you'll likely see thousands of new impressions a day. Since you're not paying for these impressions, you can think of them as free advertising for your book. Even if people aren't clicking on your ad, they are still seeing your cover, which increases your brand awareness and could very well lead to extra sales in the future.

When we talk about troubleshooting, we'll talk about the problem of starting ads that go on to get zero or very low impressions. Don't worry. It happens to all of us, and there are some workarounds we'll mention soon.

3) **Clicks.** This is the number of times somebody has clicked on your ad. When they click on your ad, they're taken to your book's Amazon sales page, where hopefully they'll go on to click the "buy" button.

4) **Click-through rate (CTR).** This is the percentage of people who see your ad and go on to click. It's calculated by the number of clicks divided by the number of impressions. If you have a great cover, your CTR will probably be higher.

There are a few things you can try to do to improve your click-through rate. A great cover (that also looks great in thumbnail) will get more clicks. This is why whenever I get a new cover design, I zoom out to see how it looks as a small image.

If you have a new release or if your title is #1 in one of Amazon's best-seller categories, your sponsored ad will sometimes appear with a little badge by it, which can also improve your click-through rate.

Some authors are concerned that an ad with a lower CTR will be deprioritized by Amazon's algorithm, so they work hard to get a lot of clicks. Since sponsored ads are so commonplace that many readers ignore them entirely, a CTR below 0.1% is nothing to worry about. I've spent significantly more than $100,000 in Amazon ads, have made hundreds of thousands back in profit, and my lifetime CTR is 0.17%.

When I look at my ads that have gotten the most lifetime impressions, my only ad that had over ten million impressions had one of the lowest CTR out of all my active ads (0.07%). Bottom line? Based on my anecdotal experience and the numbers in my dashboard, your CTR doesn't really impact how hard Amazon works to show your ad. That's why I hardly ever look at my click-through rate. It's a number you can choose to ignore.

5) **Cost-per-click (CPC).** Of much higher importance (in my opinion) than your click-through rate is your cost-per-click. This is how much you are paying Amazon each time someone clicks on your ad. There is no definition of a "good" cost-per-click, as that depends on things like your genre and your read-through rate, but when we get to troubleshooting we'll talk about what to do if your clicks are too expensive.

6) **KENP data.** If your book is in KU, the ads dashboard will show you how many page reads you get and how much in estimated royalties that calculates to. Keep in mind that these stop getting reported 14 days after a

reader clicks your ad, so if it takes a reader a month to read your KU title, you won't see ALL those page reads in your ads dashboard. A general rule of thumb is that you'll always earn more from page reads than what appears in your ads dashboard.

Remember you can customize what numbers you see when you click on customize columns so you can focus on what's important to you. If your books aren't in KU, for example, you don't need to track your KENP data. Your Amazon dashboard gives you other metrics as well. Some you can ignore, but some warrant a deeper discussion and will be covered in the remainder of this chapter.

Sales

When you view your Amazon ads dashboard, you'll see a column listing how much you've made in sales. Unfortunately, you have to do a tiny bit of math, because there is a significant difference between what your dashboard calls your sales and the amount of money that will actually appear in your bank account when royalties come due.

When I take a peek at my year-to-date data right now, I see that I've made $12,882.51 in my sales column. And although I would love for that to be the amount of money Amazon is going to pay me directly, it isn't. In fact, I'll only receive about 70% of that.

If your sales column shows $100 for a given time period, that means people have paid Amazon $100 for your books. If your book is at $0.99 cents, you'll receive 35% of that money based on Amazon's royalty breakdown. If your book is priced between $2.99 and $9.99 (and you've remembered to check the little box when you published your book to get that higher royalty percentage), you'll receive 70% of that hundred dollars.

The math gets even more complicated if you're advertising paperbacks, because you're not making an exact percentage off your paperback price. You can sell a hundred-page paperback for fifteen dollars and make seven or eight dollars profit for sale (imaginary numbers, I haven't plugged these into a royalty calculator). Someone else can sell a five-hundred-page paperback for the same price, and because production costs on the larger book are higher, only receive two or three dollars in royalties.

For right now, let's stick with the math for ebooks only. It's easier, and if you're like a lot of indie authors, you'll be selling more ebooks than paperbacks anyway.

If your book is priced between $2.99 and $9.99 and you're receiving 70% royalties, then the money you actually get to see in your bank account at the end of the royalty period is 70% of what shows up in your sales column. And that will remain the case until Amazon changes their royalty structure and gives you 100% of the sales you earn on your books. (This, of course, is never going to happen, but it's sometimes fun to dream.)

In this case, it's pretty easy to see that it's harder to make your money back on a 99-cent or $1.99 ebook because you only get 35% of royalties from those sales. This doesn't necessarily mean you should never run Amazon ads for a 99-cent book. If, for example, you have a 99-cent book that is in KU and gets you $6 or $7 or $8 every time someone downloads it and reads the entire thing (because the page count is so high), you can make incredible profit running ads on a 99-cent book. Just keep in mind that your dashboard might make it look like you're losing money out both ends since page reads are only counted for the first 14 days after somebody clicks.

Additionally, running ads on a 99-cent book might make sense if it is book one in a series that has a very high read-through rate. If you have a ten-book series and you know that every time somebody reads book one, you'll end up seeing $15 in profit for the read-through sales of all the other books in that series, then you can absolutely run ads on your 99-cent book. Your dashboard won't show you all the sales for books two through ten (so again, your dashboard will read as if you were losing money), but your bottom line could be very strong and healthy in the end.

Personally, I like to price my books at the $3.99 - $4.99 range, and I've decided that all my new releases will be at least $4.99. This gives me a profit margin that I can work with when I'm running ads, and readers don't seem to care one way or the other about that extra dollar's worth of difference.

Another thing to point out about the sales column is that this only applies to book sales made within the first 14 days after somebody clicks your ad. If somebody clicks your ad and orders your paperback three weeks later, the money you earn from that book sale does not appear in your sales column. If somebody clicks your ad then goes on to buy a different book of yours besides one that you're advertising, the money you earn from that book sale does not appear in your sales column.

Similarly, the money you earn from KU page reads does not appear in the sales data either, which is why it was such a nice gift to us when Amazon started to include the estimated money from KENP in the dashboard. (Just remember, you're earning more from KU than what your dashboard reflects because of that 14-day window. When somebody reads your KU book more than two weeks after first clicking your ad, those numbers will not be reflected in your Amazon ads dashboard.)

Cash Flow and Billing

One more quick note about your sales column, which is kind of obvious but bears discussion nonetheless, and that is a reminder that it'll take time for you to see the money you earn.

To date, the highest sales number I've seen in my ads dashboard in any given month was $8381. Since these are mostly ebooks in the 70% royalty tier, I can assume that I made $5866.70 in royalties (or 0.7 x $8381). Unfortunately, we can't access our royalty money right away. In fact, it won't appear in your bank for 2-3 months because of Amazon's payment schedule.

Some authors navigate this cash flow pinch with credit cards. If you can get a 0% interest credit card, for example, there's very little risk in paying for your August ad spend on credit, then paying off your balance when your August royalties hit your bank account at the end of October. Some authors don't like using credit or don't have access to a card, however, in which case you can grow your ad spend slowly like I did.

For the first year or so that I was running ads, my dashboard contained a lot of starts and stops. I'd spend what money I had access to, then pause my ads or lower my daily budget until more money came in. That was how I grew my ads gradually without relying on credit or going into debt, and it's absolutely possible to start by spending a couple hundred dollars a month on ads then working up to multiple thousands. Even though I didn't start my ads with credit cards, I use them now with Amazon ads for three different reasons.

1) I get a cash-back bonus from my credit cards. Since I'm going to be spending that money on ads anyway, I may as well get a kickback from it, right?

In 2021, the cash back I got was enough to pay for a new lifting machine for my husband, a hydroponic farmstand for me, and Christmas gifts for the kids.

2) Using credit responsibly with your ad campaigns can help with some of the cash flow problems I mentioned earlier. At the end of every month, as soon as you receive your royalty payments from Amazon, you can pay your credit card down to zero. Then you can run ads all month (or until your credit limit and/or my ads budget runs out) and pay it off again at the end of the next month. Basically, by using a credit card to pay for your ads, you're decreasing the amount of time between when the money you spend on ads leaves your bank and when you receive your royalty payments.

3) The first reason I started using a credit card as opposed to my debit card to run my Amazon ads actually had nothing to do with cash flow or cash-back bonuses and everything to do with the way Amazon collects payments. Amazon takes money out of your account when Amazon decides to take money out of your account. In general, I get charged for Amazon ads at the start of each month and roughly every time my ad spend reaches about $500, but there really is no way to accurately predict it.

By giving Amazon my credit card information as opposed to my debit card information, I don't have to worry about Amazon pushing out my ads like crazy and automatically taking thousands of dollars out of my bank account before I realize what's going on. Basically, if Amazon tries to bill me and that payment would take me above my credit limit, the only thing that happens is the credit card denies the charge, Amazon pauses all my ads, and the ads stay paused until I update my billing info.

I don't recommend letting this happen on a regular basis, but in my mind, a declined payment and some paused ads is a better outcome than Amazon taking thousands of dollars that I'm not expecting out of my bank account, which is what could theoretically happen if you use a debit card.

Takeaways to Remember:

- The number that appears in your sales column isn't the amount of money Amazon is going to pay you for your book. For ebooks, the amount you get paid will either be 35% or 70% of that number, depending on which royalty tier you have selected.

- It's harder to earn your money back in sales when advertising a 99-cent book; however, it can still be profitable in the end if your book gets a lot of page reads or if you're promoting book one in a series with a high read-through rate.

- Remember that even if your ads are profitable, you still have to pay Amazon for those ads a couple months before you'll see these royalties.

- There are a few compelling reasons to use a credit card instead of a debit card to pay for your Amazon ads.

Cost of Sale

To make sure your ads are earning you money and not losing you money, it's important to keep a regular eye on your ads dashboard. This doesn't have to be every day, but unless you're running just a few ads with very small daily budgets, you should check in with your data multiple times a week. This can be done on your smartphone when you have a few minutes to spare. It doesn't have to be a big production.

One metric that can give you a pretty easy idea of how well your ads are doing is the Advertising Cost of Sales (ACOS). This is an important number that gets its own column in your ads dashboard.

Your ACOS is how much money you have spent to earn one dollar worth of sales.

If your ACOS is 100%, that means you've spent $1 in ads for every $1 you've made in sales.

On the surface, it looks like you've broken even, but remember that in the ads dashboard, sales are not equal to the royalties you receive. If your ACOS is 100%, that means you've spent $1 in ads to make $1 in sales, of which you'll see either 70% or 35% depending on your royalty tier.

(Note: for the rest of this section, I'm just going to assume that we're talking about books in the $2.99 - $9.99 price range that are priced at the 70% royalty rate.)

If you're running ads on full-priced books, a good rule of thumb is to keep your ACOS close to or below 70%. A 70% ACOS on a $3.99 book, for example, means that you spent 70 cents in ads and made 70 cents back in royalties. Assuming you're promoting a book in a series and/or have page-read income in addition to sales, you've just made a profit. Even if you only write standalone books, it's not bad if your ads simply break even. Those are still sales you wouldn't have made before, and you're growing your readership so that when you write other books, you'll have ready buyers.

Bottom line is that the lower your ACOS, the more profit you've made. The temptation is strong to simply turn off any ad if its ACOS gets above 70%, but that's not always the best idea. Like I just said, if you have KU income or a series, even if you break even on ads for book one, you'll still profit from the series as a whole. I don't run ads for other authors anymore, but back when I did, if an author was in KU and had a large series, they could still be profiting in certain cases with an ACOS of 400% or higher. Here are a few other reasons to keep an ad going even with an ACOS over 70%:

1) You're promoting a new release and are okay spending a little extra money for brand awareness. Each time I launch a new book, I give myself a cushion of a few hundred dollars that I'm willing to lose in ads just to get the book out there in front of readers. These readers may go on to buy other books of mine, they may join my email list and remain faithful customers, they may leave a verified Amazon review, and they may tell their friends about my new release. At the very least, it helps my book get up in rank while it's still fresh and hot.

I'm not saying I lose money on every new book I launch, by the way. I do think we need to be responsible and not just fling out money indiscriminately so we can see our books soar up higher and higher in the charts. But I also don't kill an ad on week one if I've spent $50 and have only made back $48, because of all the other benefits I just mentioned.

This also would apply if you're trying to reach a certain sales goal, achieve a specific sales rank, or hit one of the bestseller lists. You might not make your money back right away, but if you have other goals besides making a profit (like becoming a USA Today bestseller, for example), it's okay to keep ads running with a high ACOS.

2) You're testing new ad strategies. Sometimes, it's worthwhile to run some ads just to collect data, even if those ads end up losing money in the short term. In 2018, I set a goal to sell 5,000 copies of a 99-cent novel (book one in my series) in one month, and I gave myself an advertising budget of $5,000. If you do the math, selling 5,000 copies of a 99-cent novel wouldn't bring me anywhere near earning $5,000 back, but I expected to recoup that money in series read-through. Plus, my main goal was to get data for my ads.

What I ended up doing is compiling a hundred keyword lists with a thousand words in each and running sponsored product ads to each of those lists. At the end of the month, I culled those lists for my best keywords and compiled them into a master keyword list.

About a year later, I'd spent a little over $900 and made over $3,000 in sales from that one super-ad. My ACOS is 29.67%, which is great. Based on my read-through rates, I expect that I've made close to $5,000 in royalties from that one ad alone. In this case, I don't regret losing some money while I ran those tests because the data I collected proved so valuable.

(Note: you don't have to do what I did and create massive keyword lists! However, analyzing your ads to see which keywords get you consistent sales, then compiling those keywords into a super-ad is a great idea!)

Conversion Rates

Keeping your eye on your ACOS, while it won't give you a perfect picture, is a nice way to see at a glance how a particular ad is doing. Another extremely important metric to track while you're running your Amazon ads is your conversion rate.

You won't be able to see it if you're relying on the dashboard's default column settings, but if you customize your columns and select "Orders," you'll be able to see exactly how many sales Amazon attributes to any given ad, which is an extremely useful metric for several reasons.

First of all, the "orders" column allows you to easily track your total read-through and estimated KU income. That super-ad I mentioned that contains the best-performing keywords out of a test I ran of 100,000 keywords (I must have had a lot of spare time on my hands that summer!) has 623 sales attributed to it from my ads dashboard. These are only sales of that one book, but I know from my read-through rate that for every sale of book one, I'll make around $8 back. Because I know my read-through rate and because I've customized my columns to be able to see the number of orders of that one book, I can quickly calculate that this one ad has earned me roughly $5,000 in series read-through. Not bad, considering I've spent less than a thousand dollars on clicks!

Conversion rate is another really handy metric you can calculate once you know how many orders you have from your ads. Your book's conversion rate is one of the best indicators of your book's sales potential and can help you when it comes to planning, budgeting, optimizing, etc.

Trying to run ads on your book without knowing your book's conversion rate is like trying to lose weight without knowing how much you currently weigh. Your book's conversion rate tells you how many clicks it takes for you to get one sale, and the formula to calculate it is ridiculously easy. You just take the number of clicks your ad has received, divide by the number of books in your orders column, and that ratio tells you how many clicks it takes, on average, to sell one copy of your book.

Like with anything dealing with statistics, the more data you have, the more accurate your results will be. If you've only been running ads for three days, and your ads have only gotten three clicks and one sale, it's not enough data to assume that in every case you're going to make one sale for every three clicks (although if you did manage to get that high of a conversion rate, you'd be doing really well!).

A healthy conversion rate depends on a lot of things. Asking someone to define a good conversion rate for you is somewhat like asking somebody who has no idea what you look like what a healthy weight goal for you would be. Some of my titles on Amazon have a conversion rate as low as 1:5. This means that for every five people who click on my ad, I will on average make one sale. That's quite a healthy conversion rate.

Other books have higher conversion rates, and that's okay as long as your bottom line still shows a profit. For example, my conversion rate for a three-book box set is 1:16. That means it takes 16 clicks for someone to buy one of those box sets. But since I sell these box sets at $9.99, I can afford that higher conversion. Even if I'm paying 40 cents per click, I'll still end up making a profit on that one box set alone.

The nice thing about your conversion rate is that once you know the number for your book, you can run tests to try to improve it. Changing the cover of one of my romance novels improved the conversion from 1:18 to 1:12. Before, it was difficult to get my ads to break even at the higher conversion rate. Soon, I plan to test out a new description for that book to see if I can get my conversion rate even better.

Knowing your book's conversion and being able to calculate it so simply makes it easy to test different aspects of your book's sales page to see how readers respond. Once, I changed my book's description, let my ads run for a couple weeks, and found that my conversion for that book had tanked to a 1:50 conversion. That meant it took 50 clicks to make one sale, over twice as many as it had before I made that change. Needless to say, I changed back to my previous description and then kept testing iterations of that description until that particular book's conversion rate became about 1:7. That's without making any changes to the cover, just the description!

You can (and should!) be testing and tweaking your book's creatives (like your cover and blurb) to see if you can improve your conversion rate as well. Just remember, different genres and different price points will have different conversion rates that can be considered healthy. It's more important to compare your own conversion rates to your own books, trying to constantly improve your own conversions, than to compare your books' conversion rates to other authors', especially authors outside of your genre.

We'll be talking about making improvements to your conversion rate in the following chapter. First, here are a few things to keep in mind.

Takeaways to Remember:

- The ACOS stands for your advertising cost of sales and tells you how much money you've spent to get $1 in book sales. A lower ACOS means more profit.

- Bear in mind that sales are different from royalties. If you want to make a profit on a book with a 70% royalty rate, your ACOS should be less than 70%.

- There are several types of situations in which you'll have an ACOS over 70% and still be profitable.

- Your conversion rate is the number of clicks your ad gets divided by the number of books that ad sells. You can easily calculate your conversion rate by customizing your dashboard columns to tell you the number of clicks and the number of orders your ads have received.

- You can test and tweak your book cover and sales page description and check your ads dashboard to see if those improvements have given you a better, stronger conversion rate. If you're looking at your conversion rate as a ratio (the number of clicks it takes to get one sale), then the lower your number is, the better conversion you have.

Testing to Improve Your Conversions

You've made it through the bulk of the math sections! Hopefully that wasn't too painful, and hopefully you're beginning to see how you can keep track of your ads and measure your results. (If that WAS too much for you, go back to the very simple rule of making sure that each month you make more in book royalties than you spend in Amazon ads.)

Now that you know how to measure your conversion rate, you can find different ways to try to improve it.

Remember, when we're talking about your conversion rate, we're talking about your SALES conversion. A lot of authors spend a lot of time trying to increase the number of clicks they get on ads. That's not what we're discussing here. What we're discussing here are ways to ensure that once a potential reader clicks on your ad, they are more likely to buy your book.

Think of your reader as a drop of water moving through a funnel. The first stage of the funnel is that they see your ad. If they like what they see, they will click. Your ad has one job, and that is to get potential readers to click on your book. Then Amazon will take them to your book's sales page. It is your book's sales page that does all the work from there. It's your book's cover and description (alternatively in this chapter called "blurb") that is responsible for the first step in turning a casual book browser into a buyer and an eventual lifetime fan.

Some authors spend some money on Amazon ads, get some clicks, and don't get sales. They erroneously decide that Amazon ads don't work, when in fact the Amazon ads did exactly what they were created to do — get people to click onto your book's sales page. If those readers don't buy your book after clicking, it's often a sales page issue, not an Amazon ads issue.

That's why, even though we're talking about Amazon ads, we're going to step back to discuss your sales page and how you can use the data from your Amazon ads dashboard to optimize your sales page as much as possible. The main way to do this is by testing different variables and comparing your conversion rates for each.

Running Tests

Because you've read earlier sections of this book, you now know your book's conversion rate. The formula for your book's conversion rate is the number of clicks you get divided by the number of sales in your orders column. Once you know the ratio, you can test all kinds of changes to your book's Amazon sales page to see if those changes will give you a better conversion. The possibilities of what you can test are practically endless.

As an example, I'm currently testing a new cover to see if I get a better conversion rate for book one in my romance series. (My original cover looks very wintery and doesn't sell well during the spring and summer months.) To test my hypothesis that a spring-friendly cover will improve my conversion rate, I note my conversion data for the old cover. Then I keep my ads going, still pointing to the same book and still targeting the same audiences. Now, all I have to do to see if my new cover is an improvement is compare the new results to the original cover's conversion rates.

You can get ridiculously deep into testing if you want. The most important thing to remember is that you need to collect a decent amount of data before your results will be statistically relevant. Your sales data and conversion rate will fluctuate from day to day, and it's important not to read too much into these normal variations.

The easiest way I've found to determine if the results I'm getting from a test are statistically relevant is to plug my click and sales numbers into an A/B split test calculator. You can google these, and they're very helpful. You can just type in your number of clicks and your number of sales for two different sets of data, and the calculator will tell you which variation gave you the best conversion rate and whether or not you can trust that your results are statistically relevant and not due to expected fluctuation in sales.

In this case, for test A (the old cover), I tell the calculator the number of clicks and then the number of sales my ads received before I changed my cover image. I do the same for test B (the new cover). The website does the math for me and tells me that my new cover converts better than my old cover and that my results are statistically relevant. I can rest easy now, knowing that moving to a new spring-friendly cover was a good marketing decision.

If your results aren't statistically relevant, the calculator will tell you so. That means one of two things. In one case, it means you don't have enough data. The fix is easy. Just let the test run longer and try the data again when you have higher numbers to work with. Even if you end up losing a little money in the short term, the data you might glean from these ads will often justify the expense.

Sometimes, your results will not be statistically relevant simply because the changes you made don't have a measurable impact on your conversion results. For example, if I get 100 clicks on cover A and make 15 sales, then I get 100 clicks on cover B and make 14 sales, those results are close enough to one another that I can guess my readers probably don't prefer one cover over another.

Let me give you an exaggerated example of why statistical relevance is important.

Let's say you run an ad for one of your books. You get 15 clicks and no sales. Your conversion ratio is 0, and you panic. You decide there's a problem with your book description, so you change it.

Once your new book description is published you run a new ad. On day one, your ad has received four clicks and two sales.

Wow! That looks like you've achieved a 1:2 conversion ratio. In other words, for every two clicks you receive on your ad, you get one sale. I think most of us can agree that we'd love to get results like that!

Unfortunately, you didn't let either test run long enough to get valid results. Because I'm the omniscient narrator, I know that if you had let the first ad continue to run, over time you would have seen a healthy 1:10 conversion ratio on average. And the new ad that you thought was performing so much better really wasn't. Even though you had two hasty sales right away, over time if you'd let that ad run, your conversion average would be 1:20, meaning you'd be spending twice as much money to make a sale than if you'd kept your original description. But since you didn't have the patience to let the ads run their course, you exchanged your decent description for one that didn't perform nearly as well.

Bottom line? Let your ads run and collect data before you make hasty decisions, then run your results through an A/B split test calculator online if you want to make sure they are statistically relevant.

Can you make it simpler for me, please? Not a fan of an A/B calculator? Feel like that's too reminiscent of a college statistics class? I get it. The simplified version if you'd like is to make sure you spend over $15 and/or get more than 50 clicks on anything you're testing before you make changes. That will often give you enough data to make a statistically informed decision.

Here are a few other key points to keep in mind when you're running tests on your sales page:

1) **Only change one thing at a time.** If I update my cover, my description, and my call to action on my blurb, even if I see improvements in my conversion ratio, I don't know if those improvements are from one change, two changes, or all three changes.

It's quite possible that readers love the new cover but hate the new description and call to action. Even if my average conversion shows an improvement when I change all three things at once, I don't know what's causing those extra sales.

2) **Run ads to the same audience when you're testing.** To show why this is important, let's go back to my test to see if my spring cover is a better option to use at this time of year.

If at first I'm running ads targeting readers who love legal thrillers (even though my book is a sweet Christian romance), and then after I change the cover I run ads targeting readers in my own genre, it's no surprise that I'll see an improvement in my conversion data. But I have no way to know if that improvement is because readers like my new cover better or if it's just because I'm actually targeting the right audience for this particular book.

The Amazon dashboard makes it quite easy to copy an ad, so you don't even have to go back and reenter keywords, etc. Just copy the old ad, then go into your new ad's campaign settings to give it a new name.

3) **Keep track of any changes you make on a calendar.** Any time you change your book's price, cover, description, etc., your conversion rate may (and probably will) change. It's important to keep track of these changes so you can make wise marketing decisions in the future.

For example, two months ago I had a Bookbub deal for book one in my suspense series. I marked on my calendar the date I lowered the price to 99 cents and the date I raised it back up again. I didn't stop all my ads, copy them, make new ones, and run entirely separate ads for the week and a half my book's price was decreased, but I can still determine how that price change impacted my conversion ratio.

By only selecting data for the dates when my book was on sale, I can see that book one's conversion ratio was 1:5 when priced at 99 cents. When it's at $3.99, I know it's conversion ratio is 1:8. Similarly, I can run a test to see how my conversion ratio changes if I increase the price to $4.99. My hypothesis is that the dollar increase won't make a significant difference to my sales numbers, but it can have a big impact on my total revenue. The only way to know, however, is to test.

Any time you have a sale or make changes, however slight, to your book's price or sales page, make note of that somewhere so you have data to compare it to. If you want to be super organized, you can even include what your current conversion ratio is before you make that change.

For example, a few weeks ago, I changed one of my book descriptions. I made a note on my calendar about what I changed and also jotted down what the conversion rate was for the old description. Now, I can check that against my conversion for the new description to see if my sales have improved.

Do you need to recreate all your ads when you make a change? No, that's not necessary at all, and it goes against our rule of thumb that when you find an Amazon ad that works well, don't change anything up in your ads dashboard. You can change your book description in KDP, for example, and keep all your old ads running. Then you can just compare your conversion rates before and after the change was made.

Takeaways to Remember:

- When testing, only make one change at a time.

- Make sure you collect enough data when running tests. You can use an online A/B split test calculator to verify that your results are statistically relevant, or you can make sure you've spent at least $15 and/or gotten more than 50 clicks.

- Keep track of the dates you make any changes to your book's price, cover, or Amazon description. That way you'll be able to easily track how those changes impact your conversion ratio.

How Much Should You Bid?

There are a couple different schools of thought when it comes to setting your Amazon bids. If you've already had about as much math as you can handle, I've got good news for you! One of the methods doesn't really involve math at all. To give our minds a break from calculations for a little bit (I know I'm ready for that, and I bet you are too!), let's start with what I call the "loosey goosey" method.

Loosey Goosey Bidding

If you don't feel like doing a whole lot of calculations and want to set up your ads as quickly and simply as possible, there are a few different options for your bidding.

1) **Rely on Amazon's default bids**. This goes against what you might think of since Amazon always seems out to get our money, but my ads tend to work out fine when I rely on their default bid. In fact, when I'm setting up a lot of ads at once, I often select the default bid or about five cents less than default.

When you're setting up your ad, Amazon allows you to give them a default bid, and they already have a number filled in for you. (For most of the ads I set up, Amazon's default is currently set at 75 cents.) If you want to keep things simple without doing a ton of math and testing, I recommend setting your default bid anywhere between 60% -100% of the default Amazon suggests.

2) **Use Amazon's suggested bids.** When you're targeting specific keywords, categories, or ASINs, you can choose the suggested bid option and Amazon will give you different bids for each specific target. The nice part about this is Amazon has a lot of data about which keywords are the most competitive, and they will encourage you to bid higher with these keywords while still letting you bid low for the less competitive keywords. The problem is that they may suggest really expensive bids (like over two or three dollars per click) for certain categories and keywords, and for many authors this is prohibitively expensive.

3) **Lowball it.** Some people like to start their ads with very low bids. If Amazon's default bid is 75 cents, for example, a lowball bid might be in the 20-cent price range.

Lowball bidding will ensure you're getting the absolute cheapest clicks you possibly can. The problem is your ads might never turn on. This means Amazon might never show your ads, because you've bid too low.

One option if you want to lowball it is to bid low, and if your ads don't turn on, just increase your bid by a few cents every few days until your ads start to gain impressions. If you're very patient and very budget-conscious, lowball bidding might be your best option.

Adjusting Bids as You Go

You can adjust your bid later without having to pause, end, or copy your ad. Anytime you want to make changes to your ads' bid, name, targeting options, etc. you can just click on the ad in your dashboard and it will take you to your different options. This means that there's no real pressure to choose the "correct" bid right at the start. You can start with Amazon's default or suggested bids, then after your ads have been running, you can increase or decrease your bids as necessary.

Here are a few of the scenarios where you might want to tweak your bids:

1) **Your ACOS is too high. You're losing money on your ads.** Instead of killing your ad right away, which might be the temptation, try decreasing your bid. Then measure your ad over the next week or so and see if your ACOS has gone down to a profitable number.

2) **Your ads don't turn on.** As we talked about earlier, if you bid too low, Amazon will not show your ads at all. Your dashboard will show no impressions (and therefore no clicks or sales). In this case, it's best to either increase your bid or else just start a new ad with a higher bid and see how that does. Note that up to 25% of the ads that I make (even without lowball bidding) never really turn on. Instead of stressing about it, I just make more ads. If I know I want to run a dozen ads for a specific series, for example, I might start 15 or 18 ads, keeping in mind that some of them will never turn on.

3) **Some of your keywords work well and others don't.** My most active ad (the one that's gotten me the most clicks as well as sales) is an ad I set up using 27 different genre keywords.

Some of these keywords perform amazingly for me. "Christian fiction," for example, has spent over $1,200 and earned over $2,000 in sales. My ACOS for this specific keyword is 58%.

Other keywords performed so badly I have turned them off. Before I started deliberately excluding "free" as a keyword, I was wasting money on clicks for keywords like "Christian fiction free Kindle." Since people who were hunting for free books were less likely to pay money for my novels, it's no wonder I lost money on these keywords. Thankfully, Amazon makes it easy for you to make adjustments.

If you find a keyword that isn't performing well, one option is to just pause it. Sometimes a keyword looks as though it's performing badly, but that is a result of the lag in Amazon's reporting. You can pause a questionable keyword, come back in a week, and if its ACOS hasn't improved, keep it paused. You can also archive a keyword, but that's completely irreversible, and in general I prefer pausing because it allows more flexibility.

If a keyword isn't performing badly enough that it needs to be paused or turned off, but it still isn't working quite as well as you'd like, you can decrease the bid and see what happens. I usually decrease bids by 3-5 cents and wait around a week before I try to measure any changes.

Once you find ads that are working really well for you, it might seem that increasing your bid will be the best course of action. I don't recommend this. If your ad is already running well at a 75-cent bid, why would you want to give Amazon 80 cents? So now if I have a high-performing ad, I'll increase my daily budget but rarely the bid itself.

It's important to note that the number you give Amazon for your bid is not the amount you'll be charged when someone clicks on your ad. I currently have an ad running with 65-cent bids, but my average cost-per-click is 46 cents. The bid you're giving Amazon just tells them how high you're willing to go. It's not how much you'll actually spend.

Like I said before, once you find ads that are working well and giving you consistent profit, you don't want to make too many changes, since this can upset the algorithm that determines which ads get impressions and which don't. You can absolutely make changes to an ad's name, portfolio, and daily budget without risk. But don't change a whole lot else or you might make a high-performing ad stop showing impressions.

Bottom line? The only time where it's a really good idea to increase your bid is if your ads aren't getting impressions. Once you find something that works well, an ad that gives you regular impressions, clicks, and sales, there's really no need to adjust your bid. (You may, however, choose to increase your daily budget.)

Takeaways to Remember:

- It's a perfectly fine strategy to keep bidding 60% - 100% of Amazon's default bid suggestion.
- You can lowball bid but may end up needing to increase your number if you aren't getting any impressions.
- The number you bid isn't what Amazon will charge you per click. In general, your actual cost-per-clicks will be lower than your bids.
- Once you get an ad that's working well, you can increase your daily budget but there's no need to increase your bid, and making huge changes to a good performing ad might make it lose its momentum.

Determining Your Maximum Cost-Per-Click

It's time for a little more math! If you're happy with the loosey goosey bidding method and want to stick with that, you absolutely can. It's what I do, in fact. To determine if my ads are profitable, I keep a regular eye on my ACOS as well as my ad spend versus revenue.

If you want to get more mathematical about it, however, here's how you would do that.

Once you know your book's conversion rate, you can mathematically determine the maximum amount of money you can afford to spend per click while still seeing a profit.

Let's say you get one sale for every 20 clicks, and you receive 70% of $4.99 for one sale of that book. That means for every book you sell, you earn $3.49.

Your break-even point is the amount of money you can afford to spend on one click and not lose anything. In this case, that number would be $3.49 (your royalties) divided by 20 (the number of clicks you need to make a sale). So for this hypothetical example, if you're getting 17-cent clicks, you'll break even. That means anything cheaper than 17 cents will give you a profit.

Does this mean you should only bid 17 cents a click or less? Not really. Remember, your actual cost-per-click is almost always going to be less than the bid you enter.

If, however, your ads are getting you 60-cent clicks, you may decide to pause your ad, lower your bid, or make other adjustments as necessary.

Although authors who started out with Amazon ads during the first year or so of their inception could regularly get clicks below 10 cents each, that is uncommon today for most keywords and genres. My average cost-per-click for most of my ads is around 45-50 cents. That's why it's important to account for your series read-through (if your book is part of a series) and your KU income (if your book is in KU).

Let's do that math one more time, but let's do it for a series. Let's say you have a four-book series, and you did your read-through calculation and know that for every sale of book one, you get $10 in royalties. Let's stick with the 20-click conversion rate. In this case, your break-even point is 50 cents a click (the $10 you receive for the sale of book one divided by the 20 clicks it takes you to make one sale). That's a whole lot easier to work with!

The same calculations apply with KU income for those of you with books in Kindle Unlimited. If you know that for every sale of book one, you receive $5 in royalties plus page reads, you can afford 25-cent clicks if your conversion rate is 1:20 (the $5 you receive for the sale of book one divided by the 20 clicks it takes you to make one sale).

Once you know your break-even point, you can simply adjust any ads that are spending more than that per click. You can do this by pausing the ad or decreasing your bid. You can also try to improve your conversion ratio. In the last example, let's say you improved your cover and blurb until your conversion got down to one sale for every 10 clicks. Now, you can afford 50-cent clicks in order to break even, and anything less than that spells profit.

Takeaways to Remember:

- To find out how much money you can afford to spend on one click, you need to know your conversion rate and how much money you earn (in royalties, series read-through, and/or KU income) from a single sale of book one.

- Your break-even point is how much you can spend on one click to break even. You find this number by dividing how much money you make from one sale of book one by how many clicks it takes you to sell one copy of book one (your conversion rate).

- You don't need to necessarily set your bid at your break-even point. As long as your ads are giving you a cheaper cost-per-click on average than your break-even point, your books are making a profit.

Determining Your Daily Budget

There's really no right number when it comes to setting a daily budget for your Amazon ads. I have some ads running that are doing so well, I'd be happy to give Amazon a hundred dollars a day to keep pushing those sponsored products.

But Amazon really does have a mind of its own, and since Amazon charges you per click, not per impression, it makes it very difficult to guess how much of your money Amazon will spend. Your ad spend will probably fluctuate a decent amount from day to day, which can be frustrating if you're trying to stick to a budget or predict ad spend.

The only time Amazon spends my daily budgets is if I bid at least the default bid (or higher) and have a daily budget below $10 a day. Even then, there are some days Amazon won't spend even that much.

You might think that if you're making $20 a day in profits and spending $10 a day on a certain ad, all you have to do is add a few zeroes to your daily budget. Most of us would love to spend $1,000 a day and earn $2,000 in profit, right?

Unfortunately, Amazon ads don't scale that way. If I have a daily budget set at $50 or a daily budget set at $500, I don't see any difference in how aggressively Amazon promotes that ad.

In other words, your daily budget is a useful cap if you want to start small when you're just getting your feet wet with Amazon ads. In fact, I recommend small daily budgets until you see your ads are running profitably. After that? It honestly rarely matters if your daily bid is $100 or $1,000. It's already late afternoon here in Alaska while I'm typing this, and my most expensive ad today has only spent $8.46, and that's an ad with a $500-a-day budget.

Word of warning: If you're setting daily budgets this high, remember that technically you're agreeing to let Amazon spend that much money if they choose to. That's why using a portfolio with a budget cap can be a good idea, since Amazon will automatically pause your ads after you've spent a certain amount.

Instead of increasing your daily budget, the best way to scale your Amazon ads is just to keep creating more ads and bid higher without cutting too far into your profits.

Troubleshooting and Scaling Up

At this point, you know basically everything you need to know about creating, running, and analyzing your Amazon ads. In this last section, we'll discuss a couple of potential problems you may run into with your ads, and then we get to dive into the really fun part which is how to scale up your ads when you find what works!

We're to our last chapter, but don't forget you can get a video walkthrough of the Amazon ads dashboard when you get the Amazon Ads Starter Kit for free at courses.alanaterry.com/kit[1]. I also have a full-length course on Amazon that dives into everything we talked about in this book with detailed video walkthroughs. Visit courses.alanaterry.com/amazon[2] and use coupon code AMAZONBOOK.

Troubleshooting Your Amazon Ads

As fun as they are, Amazon ads can be a little frustrating because of their unpredictability. Like I said, you might start 20 ads and only five of them start showing impressions. There's no real need to panic. It just takes patience to build up your arsenal of ads. The goal is to end up with dozens of ads running and bringing you money and new readers each and every day!

Here are a few of the most common problems you may face when running your Amazon ads.

You're not getting any impressions. In some cases, your ad just simply won't turn on. Days and even weeks after you set it up, you'll see zero impressions, zero clicks, and zero sales. There are several reasons why your ads may not turn on:

1) Your book doesn't get organic sales. Amazon wants to promote books that will sell. (Rule of thumb? Amazon wants to do what's best for Amazon!) If Amazon knows your book doesn't sell well (maybe because you have a poor cover or typos in your blurb), they're less likely to prioritize your ads. Sometimes you can jumpstart your ads by emailing your list or posting on social

1. http://courses.alanaterry.com/kit
2. http://courses.alanaterry.com/amazon

media to get a few organic sales. This will tell Amazon's AI that your book is worth promoting because people are interested in buying it.

2) Amazon doesn't have enough data. If you're trying to run an auto-targeted ad and your book hasn't made many sales recently, Amazon may not have enough data to know who to run that ad to. Try doing some keyword targeting instead, and then once you start getting more sales your auto ads might kick on.

3) You started too many ads at once. Don't ask me why this happens, but I've discovered that if I try to start twenty or thirty or forty ads in the same day, only a few of them may turn on. Try staggering your ads so they aren't all starting on the same day, which might help.

4) Your bid is too low. If your ad hasn't turned on after a couple weeks, try increasing your bid by a few cents every few days until you start to get impressions.

You're not getting any clicks. In some cases, you may be getting impressions but no clicks. In the world of Amazon ads, "a lot" of impressions is defined in the tens of thousands. A click-through rate below 1% is quite normal. However, if you have half a million impressions and still no clicks, you might want to check your targeting. Maybe your book is getting impressions, but Amazon is showing it to the wrong readers. It's also possible that something about your cover or the text you're using in your ad isn't resonating with potential readers.

You're getting clicks but no (or very low) sales. It's pretty hard to define what a "good" conversion rate is, but if you're getting 50 or more clicks and still not getting sales, something may be wrong, and one of the following suggestions may help.

1) Give it time. Don't give up after you get 15 clicks and no sales! But if you're up to 100 clicks and no sales, you might need to look at your sales page.

2) Check your description. There are lots of good resources out there for writing better book descriptions, including a few courses in the Successful Writer Academy. You can also search the Successful Writer podcast or youtube channel for our trainings on blurbs. Once you've updated your description, try running the same or a similar ad again. Hopefully, your conversion will improve and your ad will be more profitable.

3) Check your cover. This can be a more costly investment, but if you're up for testing, you can see if a new cover will lead to a better conversion rate. Since this probably means you have to hire a cover designer, I recommend working on your blurb first to see if that improves your conversion.

4) Advertise a different book. I have a few books that I don't bother running Amazon ads for. No matter how many tests I've tried and optimization experiments I've run, they just don't convert well into sales. Even if you give up advertising a particular book or series, don't give up on Amazon ads altogether. Some books are just more marketable than others.

Your cost-per-click is too high. You can have an excellent conversion rate, but if your cost-per-click is too high (especially if you don't have series read-through and/or KU page reads to help pad your author earnings), your ads still might not be profitable. The best thing to do here is gradually lower your bids by a few cents every few days (or just start new ads with a lower bid) until you reach a point where your cost-per-click is at a more sustainable level.

You might also want to check your keywords. It's possible the keywords you're using are on the more expensive side of the spectrum. Using genre keywords, for example, will often cost more than using the names of specific authors. In the same way, authors who are household names will be more expensive to target than midlist authors. If you're getting good conversions but just want to get your cost-per-click a little lower, try targeting lesser-known authors and see if that helps.

You run out of advertising money. This is where spending money to advertise your books is difficult, because you can have an ad that's really profitable, but you won't see that money in your bank account for a few months. Here are a few ways you can try to alleviate some of that cashflow pain:

1) Use a credit card (responsibly). If you have a credit card, it's very much worth considering using it for your Amazon ads in order to shorten the window between when you have to pay for the ads and when you receive your royalty check. If you can qualify for a 0% interest card, you can just pay back your ad spend when those royalties come in.

2) Put money aside each month for ads. If you really want to scale your author business, you should make ad spend one of your priorities, the way you'd spend money on book covers and professional editors. Make sure that in spite of all your other financial demands, you keep money set aside for ads. At one

point, I actually kept a separate bank account just for ads in order to ensure that money didn't get absorbed by other expenses.

3) Pause and wait. The earth won't explode if you have to pause your ads because you've reached your advertising budget for the month. Just as you should have money set aside for ads, you want to be careful that you're not spending EVERYTHING on ads either. If your ad spend gets too high one month, pause your ads until you get your next royalty payments. Your ads will be ready to turn back on when you're ready to pay. Some authors are concerned that paused ads don't do as well once you restart them; however, I've never had this problem.

Your ad is rejected. This happens more if you're in certain racier genres or if you're using a lot of text ads. Amazon will send you an email to let you know that your ad was not approved, and they'll often give you at least a clue as to why your ad was rejected. If it's not a genre issue, the second most common culprit will be grammar or spelling mistakes in your text. Sometimes Amazon is frustrating because they'll reject an ad one day but approve the exact same ad another day. The important thing is to stay calm and keep Amazon's advertising policies in mind to ensure you're in compliance.

If you're using a text-based ad, here are a few reasons your ad may be rejected: spelling or grammar errors, extra exclamation marks, words in all caps, claims of bestseller or award-winning status, or reference to prices or reviews. Here are other reasons your ad may be rejected that don't have to do with your text: your book's in a super steamy genre (you can resubmit, but sometimes Amazon just won't accept it), weapons on the cover pointed at the reader, drug references, the person responsible for reviewing your ad forgetting their coffee, or Amazon's AI developing sentience and deciding they hate you.

If you know what to fix, find your rejected ads in your drafts folder, fix the mistakes, and resubmit. If you don't know why your ad was rejected in the first place, I suggest waiting a few days to weeks, then creating a similar ad and seeing if that goes through.

Most Common Mistakes

Because we only have a few more paragraphs together before we part ways, I'd like to share this list of common mistakes that authors make with Amazon ads.

1) **You turn off keywords too soon.** Some authors kill a keyword after it gets them two or three clicks and no sales. Since there are virtually no books that have a 1:2 conversion rate, turning an ad off this soon makes no sense. Please make sure that you give a specific keyword 30 or 40 clicks before you determine if it's a dud.

2) **You pay too much attention to your click-through-rate.** Some authors waste a lot of time and energy trying to increase their CTR for their ads. Since you only get paid when someone clicks your ad and all those impressions are just giving you free advertising, there's no need to do this. Some authors worry that Amazon will deprioritize ads with lower CTRs, but some of my highest impressions ads have CTRs significantly lower than my average rate. In my experience, your CTR and your ads' efficacy are pretty much unrelated.

3) **You're too impatient for your ads to turn on.** It's rare to create two ads and have those two ads both turn on and pump out a profit. More likely, you'll create dozens of ads. A couple will work great, a couple will lose you money, and some will never turn on. There's no need to worry if you have a chunk of ads with no or few impressions. That's why we just keep making ads.

4) **You spend too much time curating keywords.** At one point, I was searching Bookbub deals and the Amazon bestseller list multiple times a week to find authors and books to target. While this is a great way to start your ads, you certainly don't need to go as overboard as I did and compile a hundred thousand different keywords to test! Now, my keyword ads usually have two dozen keywords or so, which makes them a lot more manageable, and it also ensures I'm only using the most specific targets.

5) **You blame Amazon ads for mistakes with your cover and blurb.** The only thing that Amazon ads can do for you is to get people to click onto your sales page. At that point, it's up to your sales page to actually sell your book. If you're getting one or two sales for every hundred clicks, it's most likely that your ads aren't at fault. Your sales page just needs some TLC.

Scaling Up your Ads

The best problem you can encounter with Amazon ads is when you're consistently making a profit and are now ready to turn that into an even larger profit!

With some ad platforms (I'm looking at you, Facebook!) all you need to do to scale up your ads is to increase your daily budget. But like we already discussed, increasing your daily budget after a certain point isn't likely going to do much to get Amazon to show more of your ads, and you don't want to increase your bids once you find something that's working.

This leads to a unique but good problem to have. How do you go about scaling up your ads?

1) **Copy your ads that are working well.** About once a month, I go in and look at my top-performing ads. These are ads that in general are spending upwards of $50 in a month and giving me a good profit. There's a little copy button I like to click that allows me to make a second ad just like it. That button has become a great friend of mine.

When you copy an ad, you have the option to pause the original ad or keep it running alongside its clone. I keep them both running. A few years ago, conventional wisdom around the author space was to try to avoid having ads with the same targets for the same books. My experience has been that it's totally fine to have similar (or even duplicated) ads running for the same book or series, and it's one of the best ways to scale up.

A quick word of warning: Don't give yourself a headache trying to figure out the reason for why sometimes a specific target works well with Amazon ads and sometimes that same target doesn't. For example, I have one auto ad with a 57 cent bid giving me an 82% ACOS for book one in a series. When I copied that ad, I created a clone (same bid) that spent over a thousand dollars and also gave me an 82% ACOS. When I copied the ad another time (since I was having such good success with it), I started losing money and turned that campaign off.

Similarly, sometimes in my ads analysis when I look at specific keywords, I'll notice that a keyword like "Christian mystery" gets me amazing results but "Christian mysteries" loses money. Even more confusing and potentially frustrating is I might have another campaign for the same book where the results are exactly flip-flopped. I don't spend a ton of energy trying to explain to myself why Amazon ads perform the way they do. I just take what's working, and do more of that, which is basically the primary rule for scaling up your ads.

2) **Compile your best keywords to make a super-ad.** Any time you want to see how a specific keyword is performing, you can click on the ad in question,

go to targeting, and take a peek at each keyword's individual performance. One of the most effective things you can do is make a list of your best-performing keywords for a book or series and compile those into a super keyword ad. For example, let's say I have six keyword ads going for my Alaska suspense series. Each ad has about two dozen keywords.

After I gather enough data (at least $10 per keyword, preferably more), I can take the best three or four keywords from each ad and put those keywords into one super-ad. Since these keywords have already proven how well they work, you can afford to bid a little more aggressively with your super-ad. Some of my longest running ads were created this way.

A few warnings, however, about analyzing individual keywords: First, don't turn this into something that steals hours of your life away on a daily or weekly basis. You have better things to do! Next, don't judge your keywords too quickly. Some people will turn off a keyword that has gotten five clicks and no sales. But remember, a lot of books require twenty or more clicks to get a sale. Give your keywords a chance to prove their quality. I like to make sure they've spent at least $10 before deciding if they're a "good" keyword or not.

When you have a keyword you want to stop using, I recommend pausing it, not archiving it. When you archive something in your Amazon ads dashboard, it's impossible to make changes should you choose to in the future.

3) **Try new formats and advertise internationally.** Once you're confident with sponsored product ads, go ahead and try the sponsored brand (headline) ads. The set up and targeting are basically the same. The only difference is you'll upload an author photo, select multiple books to show at once, and add a tiny bit of text.

You can also start running ads in the other English-speaking Amazon stores like Canada, UK, and Australia. If you're feeling even more adventurous, you could advertise in some of the other stores as well.

4). **Make more ads.** It's not necessarily the most exciting answer, but the other way to scale up your ads is just to keep making more of them. As you gather more and more data, you'll notice what types of ads get you the best results. (For me, my top two ads are auto ads and keyword ads targeting myself.) Once you know what's working well, keep making more of those!

In the past, authors would tell you otherwise, but it's absolutely okay to have multiple ads going for the same book that use the same type of targeting.

For example, I currently have 15 auto ads running right now for the same series. Some of these have different bids. Some have the same bids (because I just copied my ads that were working well). Bottom line? You can make a lot of ads and don't sweat about repeating yourself.

The Amazon ads platform is on record stating that your ads will not compete against each other, which means if you have two ads both targeting the keyword "military sci-fi," those two ads will not drive the bid up against each other. That's good news.

The one thing you do want to avoid, like we discussed earlier, is starting dozens and dozens of ads on the same day. That does sometimes seem to make your ads compete with each other for attention, and fewer of your ads may turn on. If you'll be making more than about twenty ads in a sitting, I recommend you stagger the start dates so they aren't all beginning at once.

I'm currently advertising about six different series, and I have 95 active ads. Over the last several years, I've created 951 ads, which means that right now 10% of the ads I created are still running. Ads don't have a shelf-life per se. Some of the ads I have running now have been working for me since early 2019. But some of the ads I created lost money and got turned off. Some of them performed well for a time and then started to lose money or stopped showing impressions. There are other ads that never turned on at all. In fact, 317 of the ads I made (roughly a third of them) have fewer than 1,000 impressions.

So remember, Amazon ads are about patience, testing, finding what works, and doing more of that. Don't feel like you have to constantly be coming up with new and fresh keywords. Just figure out what types of ads get you profit, and make a lot of those!

It should go without saying (but I'll mention it anyway!) that once you find things that don't work, you can absolutely stop doing those things. I rarely create category ads anymore, because they simply aren't worth my time. Looking at my dashboard right now, it looks like I created three category ads in 2020, one in 2021, and none in 2022. For some authors, however, category ads might be your best targets, in which case you may end up with a dozen active category ads promoting the same series.

It should come as a bit of encouragement to know that there aren't many things you can do to "break" your Amazon ads. The dashboard is quite forgiving. When you find things that work, they tend to keep working for quite a long time. So enjoy your Amazon ads and here's to you making a lot more money and selling a lot more books!

Frequently Asked Questions

It's exciting yet bittersweet to come to the end of this book. (Bittersweet for me, at least, seeing as how I still haven't written the introduction, which is the part I've been avoiding!)

Before we close up our time together, here are a few extra questions you may have about Amazon ads. Remember, if anything still doesn't make sense or if you're ready to dive into our full course spelling everything out in quite a lot more detail, go to courses.alanaterry.com/amazon[3] for my full-length course and use the coupon code AMAZONBOOK!

And now, without any further ado, it's time for some FAQ!

Should I run Amazon ads for free books? There are a few times that running ads on a free book could be a good idea. If your goal is to do a lot of keyword research, for example, and see what keywords get you a lot of clicks, it could be money well spent.

Running an ad for a free book can also be a good idea if you know that you'll gain that money back in series read-through. One quick word of warning: When I price book one in a series at free or 99 cents, my readthrough between book one and two drops significantly. Readers are notorious for downloading free books they never read, and if your book is at 99 cents, you might attract readers who are unwilling to pay full price for your backlist books. You will need to measure your results yourself to determine what price point gets you the best readthrough and profit margins.

Should I advertise my paperbacks, ebooks, or both? In general, I like to advertise an entire series at once. This includes ebooks, paperbacks, and box sets all in the same ad. It's a nice way to save a bunch of time and use the keywords, etc. that I know work.

So the short answer is go ahead and advertise your ebooks and paperbacks together. There are authors, however, who would rather get perfectly clear data, and advertising paperbacks makes it harder to figure out your royalties based just on the number of sales in your ads dashboard.

---

3. http://courses.alanaterry.com/amazon

For me, I'd rather make $100 and have some murky data than make $75 and have great data, but if the idea of lumping your books all together like that in one ad is distasteful, I recommend you advertise your ebooks in one ad and your paperbacks in another, with more emphasis on making ads for your ebooks.

Why do you recommend advertising a whole series, even if readers will start at book one? I'm all for doing what saves me time, but only if that also makes me money. Thankfully, when it comes to advertising an entire series in one ad, the simple way is also the way that gets me the most profit.

Advertising an entire series is great for brand awareness since it gets more of your book covers on one page, and the ads I create selling my whole series are just as profitable (sometimes more so!) than they were when I just advertised one book.

Having your entire series advertised may also help you get more accurate sales data. If I make an ad for book one and a reader clicks on it and goes on to buy book 2 (because they've already read book one), that sale won't show up in my ads dashboard because it wasn't a sale for the book being advertised. But if I advertise the entire series and a reader clicks an ad for book 5 but actually buys book one, that purchase is more likely (albeit not guaranteed) to show up as a sale in my ads dashboard.

How long should I let my ads run? At times you may notice that some of your ads have a "shelf life" so to speak, and after a few weeks or months they stop giving impressions or they become less profitable until you decide to kill them. Many other times, however, you'll set up ads that will just keep running and working well for you for months or even years! These ads you can keep running as long as they are profitable for you and serving your marketing goals. That's another reason I'm not a fan of setting an end date for your ads. When you find something that works, it will often keep working for quite a while!

What should I do if my ad stops showing impressions? If one of your ads was active for a while and then it stops receiving impressions, that ad has in effect "turned off." You can keep it on if you want (no harm if it's not spending money, and it could always turn back on). You could also try increasing the bid slightly, but my suggestion is to just create a second ad with the same targets and let the new one work for you instead. Every quarter or so, I'll pause anything that hasn't shown any impressions so my dashboard isn't completely cluttered with dead ads.

How many ads should I have running at one time? That's entirely up to you, your budget, and what's working well. I try to have a minimum of a dozen active ads per series. These are ads that are giving impressions AND getting me sales and profit. Sometimes I need to create two or three dozen ads before I find the ones I want to keep. This is a platform that requires some patience, as we've said, but the results really pay off in the end.

How long will it take before I see measurable results? The answer to that question will vary for each author. You might set up ten ads and a month later have only a handful of impressions and two or three clicks. Alternatively, you might create one new ad for a series that starts bringing in hundreds of dollars a week from the very first day. The best way to get good results with your Amazon ads is to keep making new ads, culling the ones that don't turn on or don't bring in profit, and keep the ones that are working well.

How much money should I devote to ads? First, you should figure out your goal. Is it to make the highest profit margin possible? If so, you'll only want to spend whatever it takes to get you the highest ROI and no more. You might keep your bids a little lower to make sure you're getting cheap costs per click.

Is your goal to gain new readers? Then you might be happy spending a hundred dollars in ads and earning a hundred dollars back in royalties. Remember, even if you are only breaking even, you're gaining lifelong readers, potential reviewers, higher Amazon ranking, etc.

Maybe your goal is series read-through. When I advertise book one in my series, I can usually (but not always) break even in sales for book one. The remainder that I earn through series read-through gets treated like icing on the cake. To that end, I'm happy to increase my ad spend as long as I'm still profiting from the series as a whole.

You also need to ask yourself how much of your monthly royalty check you want to keep for yourself as profit. If your writing career is in a growth stage, it's common to pour a significant portion of your earnings back into your business, but that may not be sustainable, practical, or desirable in the long run. In 2018, I made a goal to hit over $10,000 in Amazon sales a month and was willing to spend $5,000 in ads to do so. By 2020, I slowed down my ad spend significantly because my goal was to maintain my income, not continue doubling it year after year like I had been up until that point.

If your goal is to rapidly scale up, you'll probably be investing a big chunk of your income into ads. If your goal is to grow more slowly, you can devote a few hundred dollars a month or a smaller percentage of your income to ads ... whatever matches your goals and financial abilities.

What if I just want to hire somebody to run my ads? Will you do this for me? Hiring someone who knows what they're doing to set up and manage your ad account can be money very well spent.This is not a service I'm offering at the moment, but there are other book marketing companies who can do this, and it's often a very wise investment.

What if I want to learn more directly from you? Oh, so glad you asked! If you want in-depth videos that walk you through the entire Amazon ads process from start to finish, you definitely want to check out my full-length Amazon ads coursecourses.alanaterry.com/amazon[4] and use the coupon code AMAZONBOOK. In the course, you'll see ads in action, and you'll be able to follow along as I give you a rundown of everything ads-related in real time. There truly is no replacement for a step-by-step guide, and you'll get it all in this full-length course.

"Alana Terry's course on Amazon ads is the most helpful one I've ever taken—and I've taken a lot of courses! She's knowledgeable, to-the-point, and incredibly generous with her knowledge. Enrolling just might be one of the best decisions you've made for your book marketing career yet!" ~ USA Today bestselling author Melissa Storm

See you there![5]

4. http://courses.alanaterry.com/amazon

5. http://courses.alanaterry.com/amazon

www.ingramcontent.com/pod-product-compliance
Ingram Content Group UK Ltd.
Pitfield, Milton Keynes, MK11 3LW, UK
UKHW041850190726
13854UKWH00002B/804